The Divine Beauty Parlor

Also by Meggie K. Daly

Bead by Bead: The Scriptural Rosary

For the Sake of His Sorrowful Passion: Praying the Divine Mercy Chaplet with Scripture and Art

The Divine Beauty Parlor

Rediscovering Purgatory

Meggie K. Daly

Misericordia Publishing

All Scripture verses found herein are from the New Revised Standard Version Bible Catholic Edition (NRSVCE), copyright © 1989, 1993 by the National Council of the Churches of Christ in the United States of America. Used by permission. All rights reserved worldwide.

Excerpts from the English translation of the *Catechism of the Catholic Church*, 2nd Edition, copyright © 2000, United States Catholic Conference, Inc.—Libreria Editrice Vatican. English translation of the Catechism of the Catholic Church: Modifications from the Editio Typica copyright © 1997, United States Catholic Conference, Inc.—Libreria Editrice Vaticana.

English translations of papal documents are taken from the vatican.va website unless otherwise noted.

Cover design: Hannah Linder Designs.
All images are used with permission or are in the public domain.

Copyright © 2023 Meggie K. Daly
All rights reserved. Published in 2023 by Misericordia Publishing, United States of America

Library of Congress Control Number: 2023916799

ISBN-13: 978-1-7352388-6-9 (paperback)
ISBN-13: 978-1-7352388-8-3 (digital)

Dedication

For the St. Pat's *Fab Four*:
Julianne, Bart, Linda, and Greg

A friend is one who overlooks your broken fence
and admires the flowers in your garden.
~Unknown

"My friend," said the bishop, "before you go away, here are your candlesticks; take them."[1]

Victor Hugo,
Les Misérables (1862)

Catechism or *CCC* stands for *Catechism of the Catholic Church*, 2nd ed., (Washington, D.C.: USCCB, 2000)

Absent any adjective, the word "Church" refers to the Roman Catholic Church.

Capitalization of the word "purgatory" varies by publisher. This book uses lowercase for "purgatory" while retaining the capitalization of the original source in direct quotations. The terms "pope" and "ecumenical council(s)" are lowercase unless referencing a particular pope or ecumenical council.

Quotes found within this book are either sourced from documents in the public domain or used with permission of the publisher or in accordance with "fair use" guidelines for critical commentary and historical analysis of works in theology, philosophy, and history.

All links for websites were active at the time of publication.

Contents

Preface xi

1 – PURGATORY "LOST" 1
2 – WHAT IS TRUTH? 7
    Impact of Postmodernism 8
    Truth By Way of The Three Pillars 10
        Sacred Scripture 10
        Sacred Tradition 11
        Magisterium 12
    Dogma and Doctrine 14
3 – PURGATORY'S CALLING CARD 17
    Emergence of Sin 18
    Guilt and Conscience 19
    Venial and Mortal Sin 20
    Eternal Versus Temporal Punishments 23
    Historical Development of Temporal Punishment 25
4 – JUSTIFICATION & SANCTIFICATION 27
    Theological Differences Impacting Acceptance of Purgatory ... 28
    Steps Towards an Ecumenical Understanding of Justification .. 31
5 – MODELS OF PURGATORY 33
    Divine Mercy and Divine Justice 34
    Two Theoretical Models—or One? 35
    Baltimore Catechism's Model of Purgatory 37
    The Model for a New Century 39
6 – THE "WORK" OF PURGATORY 43
    Perfection in Love 45
    Christian Anthropology, Human Experience, and Continuity of Self 48
    Forensic Justification and Its Dilemma of Sanctification 50
7 – THE HISTORY OF PURGATORY 55
    Biblical Exegesis and Apocryphal Literature 56
    Traditions and Maturation of Theological Thought 60
        The Greek and Latin Fathers (2nd-7th Century) 60
        Missionary Monks (6th-7th Century) 63
        The Scholastic Influence (12th-13th Century) 65
    Papal and Magisterial Documents 68

Pre-Dogma Documents (13th-15th Century) 68
Dogmatic Declarations (16th Century) 70
8 – INDULGENCES & THEIR CONNECTION TO PURGATORY 73
  Basics of Indulgences 75
  Communion of Saints 77
  Treasury of the Church 77
  Further Reflections and Open Questions 78
    Indulgences and Models of Purgatory 78
    Plenary Indulgences and Instantaneous Sanctification 79
  Summary Points 80
9 – THE HISTORY OF INDULGENCES 83
  Connection to Penitential Rites 83
  Indulgences and the "Holy Wars" 85
  Scholastic Clarifications (13th-14th Century) 88
  Post-Crusades 90
    Extension of Personal Indulgence to Souls in Purgatory 91
    Problems, Abuses, and Attempted Reforms 91
  Protestant Reformation and the Declaration of Dogma 93
  Prayers for the Dead Revisited 95
10 – CULTURAL EXPRESSIONS & PRETERNATURAL EXPERIENCES OF PURGATORY 99
  Medieval Art 100
  Medieval Literature 102
  Popular Opinions, Legends, and Stories 103
  Writings of the Saints 105
11 – AVOIDING PURGATORY 109
  Traditional Channels of Grace 110
  The "Little Way" 111
12 – CONCLUSION 115
  Purgatory "Found" 121

Acknowledgments 123
About the Author 125
Notes 127-155

Preface

Two teachings troubled me when the Holy Spirit called me back to the Catholic Church. One was the Real Presence of Christ—Body and Blood, Soul and Divinity—fully present, but veiled, in the Eucharist. The other was purgatory. Neither teaching had concerned me as a Protestant because neither was celebrated as truth.

The early Church Fathers, whose ministries overlapped with the apostolic age, clearly proclaimed the Real Presence and helped strengthen my faith regarding the Eucharist.[2] But belief in purgatory was quite another matter. I knew that Purgatory wasn't explicitly mentioned in the Bible. But then again, neither was the Trinity, yet all three persons (or manifestations) were present in Scripture. (cf. Mt 28:19)

The various Protestant churches I'd attended previously had no theological need for purgatory. Accepting Jesus as my Lord and Savior generated my "golden ticket" with admittance straightaway into heaven with no postmortem stopovers. When God looked upon me at my death, he would no longer see any stain of my sins but rather a pristine soul washed clean in the blood of Jesus. Moreover, I could never lose my golden ticket. "Once saved, always saved." Talk about good news!

The Evangelical Church that I had joined after my conversion experience in 2004 emphasized that it was through no action of my own that I was saved. All I needed to do was accept the free gift of salvation by saying the "Sinner's Prayer" or making a private profession of faith. As seductive as golden-ticket theology was for a sinner such as myself, I couldn't shake the niggling feeling that the theology of my new worship community was overly simplistic.

Did removing the guilt of my sin by praying the Sinner's Prayer aloud clear up sin's effect emblazoned on my will and intellect? At death, how did my battered soul regain enough spiritual health to enjoy heaven and the holiness to stand in the presence of God? Was purgatory part of that equation?

When I finally returned to the Catholic Church, I had to turn in my golden ticket and was confronted with the prospect of working out my salvation in fear and trembling. Now, the prospect of purgatory loomed large! Consequently, the purgatory that I was only too happy to kiss goodbye thundered back into my life.

But I had a ton of questions. Was purgatory a place separate from heaven or hell? Was its purpose purification of the sinner or punishment for his sins? Was purgatory a blessing or a curse? Did God send me there, or did I send myself there? Was purgatory a dogma of the Catholic Church or some optional teaching? When did Christians first start talking and writing about purgatory? Can one help those in purgatory by Masses or prayers? If so, what does that say about the function of purgatory? And what about indulgences and their reputed abuses? Does the Church still grant them? Can the souls in purgatory pray for us? Anyway, you get the idea.

In the spring of 2012, I read the *Diary of St. Faustina*. I was captivated and frightened by her "visits" to and descriptions of purgatory. Next, I ordered a DVD entitled *Purgatory: The Forgotten Souls*. I learned of Fr. Doug Lorig, a remarkable Catholic priest, through that DVD. Originally a married Episcopal priest, he was ordained as a Catholic priest in 1984.[3]

Fr. Lorig had a great sensitivity toward the souls in purgatory. Over the years, he jotted down the names of all the deceased persons for which he had been asked to pray in a little notebook. He kept this notebook with him when offering Mass.

In an interview on the DVD, Fr. Lorig relayed a "ghost" story that haunted me. During one of his young granddaughter's visits, she asked who the man was *without a mouth* standing in the backyard of the rectory. Lorig considered (rather than discounting) her question and, after some research, discovered that some years back, a priest living at the rectory had taken his own life by firing a gun into his mouth. Fr. Lorig began praying for the soul of that priest, and eventually, the visits stopped. It was this story that started me on my journey to understand purgatory.

There are many books out there on purgatory. Why should you read mine? Because I've sat on both sides of the purgatorial divide—con and pro, in that order. After worshiping with my Protestant brothers and sisters for a decade, I returned to the Catholic Church.

That experience as an Evangelical Protestant has influenced my broad approach to topics in this book. For example, this book explains the underlying theological concepts behind Catholicism's acceptance of purgatory and Protestantism's rejection.

For me, some of the most convincing logical arguments for purgatory come from Protestants. Yes, you read that correctly! Even if you accept the dogma of the Catholic Church, and I do, purgatory's "logic of total transformation"[4] best explains how God perfects us in love to make us both capable and worthy of heaven. I believe that faith builds on reason. Asking, "Why?" humbly and honestly leads us to God, not away from him.

The Church's teaching on purgatory requires a sophisticated understanding of several catechetical concepts that not every reader may possess. This book remedies that situation without any prerequisite knowledge beyond the basics of Christianity. You do not have to be a theologian, a philosopher, or a Catholic to follow along—curiosity is the only prerequisite. Loving history is a boon, as this book has lots of it.

Many cradle Catholics of my generation are no longer members of any Christian worship community, others fill the pews (or chairs) in Protestant churches, and some practicing cradle Catholics don't know what the Church teaches about purgatory. Other Catholics reject purgatory outright, regardless of what the Church teaches. Some Catholics have never progressed beyond an immature understanding of purgatory as a "place" of terror and punishment. Before reading the *Catechism of the Catholic Church* in 2012, I was in the latter category. Through the research culminating in this book, I have discovered purgatory as a "place" of hope and reconciliation—a gift from God who never gives up on those who love him.

For some, purgatory causes a disinterested yawn, but for others, it engenders much hostility toward the Catholic Church. In 2021, I ordered a new copy of the book *Purgatory is for Real* by Catholic apologist Karlo Broussard. When I opened the book, I found a "love" note on the title page written by the previous purchaser, who must have returned the book to the online retailer as new. The retailer then sent me the marked-up copy. The man, who signed his full name and dated his comments, left these thoughts for me:

> *Reading this book I felt a sense of mostly Catholic opinion—a whole lot of 'reaching.' One thing is true; the idea of purgatory is definitely a very lucrative business for the Catholic Church.*

The previous owner had highlighted two quotes inside the book. The first was from Peter Mogila (1597–1646), a famous Orthodox Christian theologian highly critical of the Latin Church, who rejected purgatory because Scripture makes no mention of it. The second highlight was a quote after Martin Luther came to reject purgatory as the work of the devil.

I thank Mr. J___O____ for returning his marked-up copy of *Purgatory Is for Real* and for sharing his thoughts with me. He helped motivate me to turn my personal research into this book.

While not a theologian, philosopher, historian, or Catholic apologist, I am a researcher who asks questions until I understand at the "ground-floor" level. This book is the result of my quest.

I hope you will rediscover the perfect reasonableness of purgatory and prayerfully ponder that mysterious "bridge" that connects the presence of sin in the individual to the personal call to holiness necessary for union with God. Enjoy!

1 – PURGATORY "LOST"

Many believers have attended funerals in which the deceased are declared to be enjoying all the glories of heaven, regardless of their somewhat less-than-saintly behavior in life. At best, such occasions are examples of understandable pastoral efforts to comfort grieving loved ones. But at worst, they may be sentimental exercises that trivialize the most central beliefs of the Christian faith.[5]
    Jerry L. Walls, Protestant Philosopher

Decades ago, theologian Karl Rahner, S.J., wrote that some truths in the Catholic Church are being "silenced to death" because no one cares enough to dispute them. While still found in the *Catechism*, these truths are absent from religious practice and "not inscribed *in our hearts on tablets of flesh.*"[6] Rahner had indulgences in mind when he penned those words, but now, some sixty years later, he could have been discussing purgatory just as well.

Where did purgatory go? Why isn't purgatory mentioned these days from the pulpit? Is purgatory still a "thing"? Am I the only one who asks these questions? I think not.

In 1995, the Los Angeles Times ran an article entitled "Purgatory: After years of neglect, some Protestants now believe it exists; many Catholics don't."[7] I wondered if this had changed. A 2017 Pew Research Center survey reported that 70% of Catholics believed in purgatory, while 70% of Protestants didn't. Averaged across all survey respondents who self-identified as Christian, 42% said they believed in purgatory, and amazingly, 17% of those without any religious affiliation did as well.[8]

The Pew survey reaffirms long-ingrained hostilities toward purgatory outside Catholic culture, to which I would add the practice of praying for the dead. Many Protestant faith traditions see both beliefs as part of a "much larger system of works that undercuts free grace" that remains "ecumenically charged."[9] Discussing purgatory with any broad Christian audience is bound up with how various Christian faith traditions understand the "conceptual issues (e.g., how one understands communion with the departed or the transformation of the self between death and heavenly glory) and issues of practice (e.g., prayers, indulgences)."[10]

Purgatory is viewed by many Protestants as an insult to the salvific work of Christ, as if his redemptive work on the cross was insufficient for payment for our sins. Moreover, purgatory is inconsistent with the common Protestant belief that saving faith takes the deceased straight to heaven.

Younger Catholics may know nothing about purgatory or the related practice of indulgences. Some older Catholics wonder if purgatory is still part of Catholic doctrine, as it is rarely mentioned from the pulpit, even at funerals. Catholic scholar and theologian John Thiel reflected on an experience at his parish church in 2000 when the homilist spoke about the availability of a Jubilee Year plenary indulgence, which was never defined or connected to purgatory. Thiel hypothesized that the priest assumed that the "younger members of the congregation would not know what purgatory was and that older members had long left it behind."[11] Yet indulgences are devoid of meaning without purgatory.

To be clear, purgatory remains a dogma of the Catholic Church, and the Church never retracts its declaration of dogma. However, the Church's understanding can and does mature over time. Five years after the LA Times article splashed its 1995 "Purgatory" headline, the second edition of the English language *Catechism of the Catholic Church* was published. The section on purgatory included three paragraphs; the first (§1030) reads:

All who die in God's grace and friendship, but still imperfectly purified, are indeed assured of their eternal salvation; but after death they undergo purification, so as to achieve the holiness necessary to enter the joy of heaven.

When I first read those words in 2012, they didn't quite resonate with my nightmare-worthy recollections of purgatory from religion class in elementary school. Absent was any mention of punishment, pain, or fire. While the *Catechism of the Catholic Church* didn't rule out such unpleasantries in their "purification" concept, it said nothing about them either.

It didn't take long to find that other depiction of purgatory. One of the first books I read was Fr. F.X. Schouppe's *Purgatory Explained by the Lives and Legends of the Saint*, first published in 1893. There, I found the purgatory that I feared:

> *That fire, enkindled by Divine Justice, those excruciating pains, compared to which all the penances of the saints, all the sufferings of the martyrs put together, are as nothing, who is there that thinks he will be able to look upon them and not shudder from very fear?* [12]

The terror-laced pages of Schouppe's book were entirely consistent with the views of St. Thomas Aquinas (1225-1274) on purgatory:

> *In Purgatory there will be a twofold pain; one will be the pain of loss, namely the delay of the divine vision, and the pain of sense, namely punishment by corporeal fire. With regard to both the least pain of Purgatory surpasses the greatest pain of this life.* [13]

Martin Jugie's still-popular book *Purgatory and the Means to Avoid It*, originally published in 1950, largely reflected the thinking on purgatory from the late 13th century, emphasizing the punitive aspect over the purification aspect. Jugie's purgatory was Schouppe's "version" that I'd carried from elementary school into adulthood.

But this was not the purgatory of the *Catechism*. How did purgatory get its "makeover"? Or did it?

I learned that after the theological and pastoral reception of the reforms of the Second Vatican Council (1962-1965), purgatory seemed to all but disappear. However, the council had left purgatory's doctrinal teaching virtually untouched and unchanged since the original defining councils in the late Middle Ages.

Before Vatican II, the Church emphasized the eschatology or "last things" for the individual: death, judgment, purgatory, heaven, and hell, which dealt almost exclusively with the salvation of the individual's soul or destiny. However, Vatican II emphasized the cosmic or universal dimensions of eschatology: the end of the world, the resurrection of the body, the general judgment, and the final redemption of creation. This universal dimension bound up the destiny and hope of the individual with that of all humanity and the entire universe.[14]

This shift in emphasis on the universal aspect had implications for purgatory, too. Our personal rehabilitation, sanctification, and expiation in the afterlife took on a broader connection to the reparation of our relationships here on earth.[15] The cosmic or universal dimensions did not in any way trump the individual aspects—both are essential parts of the whole. But purgatory had been historically associated with judgment for personal sin. After Vatican II, there was as strong an emphasis on God's infinite mercy as there had been on his justice (often to the neglect of his mercy) in times past.

Some have blamed the "disappearance" of purgatory on a diminished sense of personal sin, citing further evidence in the waning reception of the Sacrament of Reconciliation in popular Catholic practice.[16] Pope Francis has warned against the desensitization of sin in both the universal and individual aspects of humanity's destiny in today's culture:

> *The process of secularization tends to reduce the faith and the Church to the sphere of the private and personal. Furthermore, by completely rejecting the transcendent, it has produced a growing deterioration of ethics, a weakening of the sense of personal and collective sin, and a steady increase in relativism.*[17]

While Catholics heard less about purgatory, some Protestant theologians and philosophers developed a renewed interest. This openness was due, in part, to the way the *Catechism* now expressed purgatory. These critical thinkers took another look at the purification function of purgatory while distancing themselves from Catholic purgatory, which included punishment for sin. But in reexamining purgatory, they confronted some glaring theological insufficiencies in their Protestant theology regarding how imperfections are removed in the soul before entrance to heaven. These philosophers of religion advanced solid arguments for some form of postmortem purification based on Christian anthropology. In other words, does human nature itself and Christianity demand some sort of postmortem purification?

But even before the *Catechism* seemingly created a new openness to purgatory, a handful of Protestant theologians argued that an intermediate state of postmortem purification or fuller conversion had a place in Protestant theology.[18]

In writing of his journey from a Pentecostal faith tradition to Anglicanism and finally to Catholicism, philosopher Bryan Cross warns against our natural tendency to interpret theology from the vantage point of our personal philosophy or the faith paradigm in which we grew up. From the onset, we often presume the falsity of the very position that (we erroneously believe) we are objectively evaluating.[19] This is especially true regarding purgatory, where historic battlelines are hard and fast, and the topic is a theological muddle of multiple topics, some unpleasant history, and nontrivial theology compounded by animosity and misunderstanding.

When we grasp the theology *underlying* the disagreement between Catholics and Protestants regarding purgatory, that understanding enables respectful ecumenical discussions. Indeed, in a time such as this, when the light of Christianity seems to be burning dimly in the public and political spheres, the glue that binds all Christians together should unite us more than what divides us. Our common bond in Christ Jesus is strengthened when we understand our philosophical and theological differences.

The remaining eleven chapters of *The Divine Beauty Parlor* fall into four broad categories, as briefly described below. The chapters build upon one another. Chapters 2 through 4 provide important background for the remaining chapters. So, hang in there as you are reading should you think, "What does this have to do with purgatory?" Trust me, it does.

Many Christians deny purgatory because of past abuses of indulgences. However, rejecting indulgences is theologically and philosophically independent of accepting purgatory.[20] The Church has linked indulgences closely to her teaching on purgatory. I have treated indulgences theologically and historically in this book for these reasons.

General Background and Terminology
- Chapter 2: Assault of modernism and postmodernism on metaphysical truth; Paradigm used by the Catholic Church to assert truth and proclaim dogma; Difference between dogma, doctrine, and theology.
- Chapter 3: Theology of sin; Differentiation between eternal and temporal punishment; Meaning of temporal punishment due to sin; Historical evolution of the Church's teaching on venial and mortal sin and temporal punishment.
- Chapter 4: Differences between Protestant and Catholic doctrines of justification and sanctification, and the implications for purgatory; Ecumenical steps towards consensus.

Doctrinal Teaching and Theological Thought
- Chapter 5: Conceptual models of purgatory; Catholic dogma of

purgatory; Changes in catechetical emphasis in the last two centuries.
- Chapter 6: Theological study and reflections on the "work" of purgatory; Christian anthropological insights from Protestant theologians and philosophers of religion.

<u>Historical and Cultural Background</u>
- Chapter 7: Hints and history of purgatory, beginning with early Christians through the Council of Trent to dogmatic declarations.
- Chapter 8: Basics of indulgences; What they are and aren't; Their connection to purgatory.
- Chapter 9: History of Indulgences from the early Church's penitential rites through the Middle Ages and to modern times.
- Chapter 10: Cultural manifestations of purgatory in the arts; Supernatural experiences reported by Catholic saints associated with visions of and visitors from purgatory.

<u>Looking Forward</u>
- Chapter 11: Spiritual "advice" on ways to avoid purgatory, borrowing from the wisdom of the Church, her theologians, and the words of her saints.
- Chapter 12: Putting it all together—the culmination of my research and personal thoughts.

2 – WHAT IS TRUTH?

Faith and reason are like two wings on which the human spirit rises to the contemplation of truth; and God has placed in the human heart a desire to know the truth—in a word, to know himself—so that, by knowing and loving God, men and women may also come to the fullness of truth about themselves. [21]
Pope St. John Paul II

Any discussion of purgatory will never make sense unless one understands how the Catholic Church defines truth, dogma, and doctrine. The Catholic paradigm to discern truth includes Scripture, Tradition, and the Magisterium (the Church's teaching authority comprised of the pope and bishops in union with him). This paradigm is distinct from Protestant faith traditions that are based solely on the exegesis of Scripture. However, exegesis is not an "entirely objective activity," as it tacitly imports "many philosophical and theological assumptions in the process."[22]

When I took philosophy classes as an undergraduate, the search for truth and "knowability" rested upon Aristotle's principle of non-contradiction: "It is impossible for anyone to suppose that the same thing is and is not"[23] or simply, a thing cannot *be* and *not be*. Philosophy and mathematics rest on this principle, as does theology, the religious branch of philosophy. For this reason, most theologians have a solid background in philosophy and assert that God, as Absolute Truth, cannot act in contradiction to his nature.

The Catholic paradigm for discerning truth and specification of dogmatic statements of faith contrasts sharply with our modern culture's philosophical frame of reference and mode of dialogue.

Impact of Postmodernism

We live in a period of history called postmodernism that began around the mid-20th-century.[24] Postmodernism has influenced art, literature, architecture, philosophy, ethics, morality, and governmental laws and policies. Although defying simple descriptions, most historians agree that it is a system of thinking characterized by a general suspicion of reason; postmodernism denies objective universal truth and absolute moral values.

Postmodernism followed a period called modernism, roughly 1700-1850, in which "truth" was discovered by pure reason and empirical methodology. Modernism initiated the demise of the metaphysical and the spiritual.[25] That which was not observable and open to the scientific method of testing and verification wasn't accepted as true in modernism. The problem with modernism was that it extrapolated the scientific method outside its natural sphere of application. It denied what elevated human beings above animals and nature: his soul.

The death of metaphysical truth ushered in by the modernist period was further generalized to include scientific truth in the postmodernist period. In the postmodernist paradigm, all truth becomes relative and is determined by the individual. My truth and your truth may contradict one another, yet both are embraced as true and equally valid. The fact that this contradicts reason is not a problem for the postmodernist, for he implicitly rejects the principle of non-contradiction.

A postmodernist view is that gender is independent of biology. Gender becomes a social construct determined by the individual. To restrict an individual's right to euthanasia or abortion (even up to live birth) becomes bigotry because it is an imposition of one person's view of truth upon another and restricts what is morally permissible by the ethical system of the other.

Knowledge is replaced by information for the postmodernist. The possibility of knowledge is questioned or simply denied. The epistemology[26] of postmodernism is inconsistent with the principle of identity, which asserts that truth has an absolute and atemporal character. Christian dogma, doctrine, teaching, and theological inquiry operate on the principle of identity in its declaration and pursuit of absolute and atemporal truths.

Postmodernism has percolated through several generations in

our universities and has made its way into our school system at all levels. Having redefined "truth," this philosophy has imprinted its mark in the hearts and minds of two generations. It is as insidious as it is deadly to Christianity.

To deny any absolute or objective truth is to deny the Christian God and the foundation of Christianity. Jesus said he was the way, the *truth*, and the life. (cf. Jn 16:6) He did not say he was some version of the truth for me but a different one for you. Under the "jurisdiction" of relativism, speaking Christian "truth in love" becomes bigotry.

We see this philosophy in the "Catholics for Choice" movement, which claims that they represent 68% of Catholics[27] and base their views on a misconstrued post-Vatican II freedom of conscience.[28] Freedom of conscience presumes a properly formed conscience and does not trump the teachings of the Church.

From this postmodern context, perhaps we should not be surprised that for many self-identified Christians, discerning what is good and what is evil or moral becomes too complicated, if not impossible. A 2021 Pew Research Study asked subjects to complete a sentence with one of two sentiments: Most things in society a) can be pretty clearly divided into good and evil or b) are too complicated to be divided into good and evil. Of those who responded, 71% self-identified as Christian. Catholic respondents were split down the middle (49% versus 49%). Protestants felt slightly more confident in discerning good from evil (56% versus 41%). Some Christians did not answer at all. For those with no religious affiliation, 62% said it was too complicated.[29]

Apparently, in the postmodernist period, we all get to answer the question for ourselves that Pilate asked Jesus two thousand years ago, "What is Truth?" (cf. Jn 18:38) Or do we? Do we believe God's definition of truth and morality is as elastic as ours? Perhaps our shared mortality is the last truth we, as a society, can collectively embrace.

In the same 2021 Pew survey, three out of four people reported belief in some kind of afterlife, and four out of five believed in near-death experiences.[30] Yet, as a society, we insulate ourselves from death as much as possible. We no longer have funerals; we have celebrations of life. How different might we live if we saw earthly existence as a drop in the bucket of eternity?

Irish theologian Dermot A. Lane wrote that it is "only when we have faced the question of death and accepted death in all its ambiguity that we have fully understood who God is and have come to grips with who we are."[31]

Either God has ordained purgatory for his good purposes, or he has not. When we die and enter eternity, a personal rejection (or acceptance) of purgatory does not alter God's plans for us. We may not know many details about purgatory, but it does not keep us from wondering and asking questions—a good thing! Questions prayerfully directed to God help us walk toward him.

While purgatory may be "silenced to death," it remains a dogma of the Catholic Church. But what does *dogma* mean, and how is it defined? Must Catholics accept all dogma the Church proclaims, including purgatory? Is there a difference between dogma, doctrine, and theology?

Truth By Way of The Three Pillars

The Catholic Church asserts truth using Scripture, Sacred Tradition, and the Magisterium. Scripture and Tradition work in concert to unveil the Word of God. The Magisterium, composed of the pope and bishops faithful to him, stands in service to the teaching ministry of the Word.

Sacred Scripture and Tradition are considered a single sacred deposit of the Christian faith given by Christ and the Holy Spirit to the Church. The Catholic Church provides her faithful with teachings based on revelation in Scripture, the Magisterium, and Tradition.[32]

Sacred Scripture

All Christians accept the Bible as the inspired Word of God and that the Holy Spirit inspired its human authors.[33] Since the time of Martin Luther, *sola Scriptura* (the Bible alone) has separated Protestants from Catholic and Eastern Orthodox Christians.[34] Since the word *purgatory* never appears in the Bible, that is enough for many Christians to reject purgatory outright. While praying for the dead does appear in the Old Testament, that particular book, 2 Maccabees, is not included in Protestant versions of the Bible.[35]

From the Protestant perspective, *sola Scriptura* means that the Bible alone is the supreme authority in all spiritual matters and that everything needed for salvation is contained in its pages. Each individual, under the guidance of the Holy Spirit, can discern sacred truths. Given a *sola Scriptura* approach to discerning truth, the role of tradition and an overarching, magisterial spiritual authority is unnecessary.[36]

The 73 accepted books (or scriptural canon) of the Catholic Bible were formalized first in 382 by the Council of Rome, and were left unchanged by several regional councils and ecumenical counsels.[37] Martin Luther (1483-1546) introduced the first change to the scriptural canon. The revised Protestant Bible deleted seven books: Tobit, Judith, 1 Maccabees, 2 Maccabees, Wisdom, Sirach, Baruch, and several parts of Daniel and Esther. The second book of Maccabees will be important later in the discussion of purgatory and prayers for the dead.[38]

The New Testament canon remained the same for Martin Luther's new canonical classification. However, Luther segregated the New Testament books of Hebrews, James, Jude, and Revelation into an appendix because they did not wholly conform to his theology. The book of James was Luther's least favorite. Perhaps because James 2:24 reads "that a person is justified by works and not by faith alone." [39]

Sacred Tradition

In 1 Timothy 3:15, Paul wrote, "If I am delayed, you may know how one ought to behave in the household of God, which is the *church* of the living God, the *pillar* and *bulwark of the truth*" (emphasis added). In apostolic times, there was no New Testament to draw upon. The early Church based its teachings on what Christ taught his apostles and the traditions they passed down before the canon of the Bible was formalized.

The Church distinguishes between Sacred Tradition ("big T") and ecclesial tradition ("little t"). Ecclesial traditions can and have changed over the Church's history, while Traditions do not change.

Changing the Mass from Latin to the language of the people post-Vatican II is an example of an ecclesial tradition that has changed. No longer requiring Catholics to abstain from meat every Friday but allowing another form of penance to commemorate

Christ's death is another ecclesial tradition. That bread and wine become the Real Presence of Christ during the consecration at the Mass is an example of Sacred Tradition and is fundamental to the Catholic faith.

Before the New Testament came together, the Church depended on the oral teachings and traditions of the apostles, passed on to those they instructed under the guidance of the Holy Spirit. Before the Bible was a "bible," Sacred Tradition was the glue and the guide. Scripture and Tradition are tightly coupled. St. Paul wrote, "So then, brothers and sisters, stand firm and hold fast to the *traditions* that you were taught by us, either by word of mouth or by our letter." (2 Thes 2:15)

But what happens when disagreements occur in interpreting Scripture or Tradition or tradition, as is bound to happen? After all, this Deposit of Faith is housed in weakened earthen "vessels"—us.

Magisterium

When Christ was on earth, his apostles could ask him about his revelations. After his death, they had to answer their new disciples' questions by themselves and decide about things they had never considered before. Recall the Acts of the Apostles (15:1-29). At issue was whether Gentiles had to be circumcised to become followers of Jesus. In other words, did they have to become Jewish first?

Paul sought guidance from the other apostles. They all gathered during the First Council of Jerusalem to decide the matter, with Peter finally settling the issue once and for all:

> *The apostles and the elders met together to consider this matter. After there had been much debate, Peter stood up and said to them, "My brothers, you know that in the early days God made a choice among you, that I should be the one through whom the Gentiles would hear the message of the good news and become believers. ... Therefore I have reached the decision ... "*

How the Catholic Church decides binding issues of faith and morals has not changed since apostolic times.[40]

The role of the Magisterium is to continue the teaching and prophetic mission of the Church entrusted to the apostles. Protestants do not deny Peter's role in leading the apostles, nor what happened during the First Council in Jerusalem. However, they would argue that with the death of the apostles and Peter, the office of primary authority given to Peter ended, which is why Protestants reject papal authority.

Catholics believe that, over time, the Church's understanding of the divine revelation becomes clearer under the guidance of the Holy Spirit. The truth doesn't change, but our understanding continues to deepen. This most often happens during councils with bishops present from all over the world under the leadership of the pope.

While upholding the philosophical *principle of identity*, Karl Rahner, S.J., one of the most influential theologians of the 20th century, believed that human understanding of concepts is "always time-bound" and that all theological truth is capable of "deeper understanding, appreciation, and development."[41] He wrote that "[a]nyone who takes seriously the historicity of human truth (in which God's truth, too, has become incarnate in Revelation) must see that neither the abandonment of a formula nor its preservation in a petrified form does justice to human understanding."[42]

Rahner's words may be applied to the Magisterium's challenge to safeguard the truths of the Christian faith, to speak them with a timely relevance and responsiveness, yet protected from the assaults to truth (i.e., heresy) from the earliest times to the present day. The first Ecumenical Council took place in Nicaea (325 AD), which affirmed the two divinities of Christ (fully God and fully man) in response to the Arian heresy and produced the Nicene Creed.[43]

The dogma of the Trinity exemplifies how our understanding of Revelation becomes fuller with time. Consider that the word "Trinity" is found nowhere in the Bible. Yet Christians of all denominations agree that the Trinity is three persons in one God.[44] It took several centuries and heated debate to develop the terminology to articulate this greatest mystery of the Christian faith with any precision. The Second Council of Constantinople (553 AD) officially formalized the central mystery of the Christian faith.[45]

In summary, the Magisterium is the guardian and servant of what has been revealed by the Word of God through Scripture and Tradition. It is the continuation of the apostolic authority given to the office of the apostles, handed down through the centuries through Holy Orders from the apostles.

We moderns wrestle with many issues never conceived of during biblical times: in vitro fertilization, morning-after pills, and same-sex marriage, to name a few. The Church is responsible for speaking out on such moral issues, using biblical principles and Tradition, with the guidance of the Holy Spirit. The Magisterium is her mouthpiece.

The Protestant paradigm for resolving theological differences rests entirely on the exegesis of Scripture, where each person led by the same Holy Spirit can (and often does) arrive at different (and inconsistent) interpretations. The Catholic paradigm is different, relying on Tradition and the Magisterium in the absence of scriptural clarity.[46]

Christians often disagree in matters of faith and morals, purgatory being a case in point. If our interpretation of Divine Revelation is not to degenerate into a cacophony of inconsistent versions of the "truth," there has to be an authority to discern the voice of the Holy Spirit above the noise.

Before converting to Roman Catholicism, John Henry Cardinal Newman (1801-1890) recognized that each person deciding the truth for himself could only lead to chaos. For Newman, conscience was the voice of God—where we encounter God. But he did not trust pure reason in matters of religious truth.[47] He recognized the wisdom of an overarching authority.

Absent the pillars of Tradition and Magisterium, Protestantism has fragmented into thousands of denominations, with differences and incompatibilities in theological interpretations largely to blame. Without an overarching authority, *sola Scriptura* opens up every debate or heresy in the early centuries of the Church without the opportunity for closure.[48]

Dogma and Doctrine

The Catholic Church distinguishes between her extraordinary Magisterium and her ordinary Magisterium. The ordinary Magisterium teaches in matters concerning faith and morals, but only the extraordinary Magisterium declares dogma.

> *The Church's Magisterium exercises the authority it holds from Christ to the fullest extent when it defines dogmas, that is, when it proposes truths contained in divine Revelation or also when it proposes in a definitive way truths having a necessary connection with.*[49]

Dogma is defined as a truth God reveals through Scripture and Tradition, which the Magisterium has declared as binding. Dogma comprises the essentials of the Christian faith. The Trinity and the Incarnation of Christ are two such dogmas. Dogma runs counter to the relativism of postmodern times, where each person decides on their version of the truth.

Doctrine is the Church's teaching regarding dogma. Doctrine is not directly revealed by Christ or Scripture. Doctrine and dogma are often used interchangeably, but there is a subtle difference. A single dogma could generate several doctrines. Catholic doctrine consists of teachings concerning faith and morals taught by the Magisterium, ordinary or extraordinary.

The Bible contains many truths recognized as doctrine, which the Church has not defined as dogma. Historically, ecumenical councils formalized doctrines as dogmas to combat heresies. This was the case with purgatory.

All dogma is doctrine, but not all doctrine is dogma. Dogma is more narrowly defined. Faithful Catholics are called to believe in doctrine (which includes dogma). Two kinds of arguments support Catholic doctrine: authority and fittingness. Authority appeals to the "teaching of Christ and the apostles, as interpreted by the Church," while fittingness appeals to consistency with "God's character and past revelation."[50]

The *Catechism* does not present a concise list of all dogmas, but it does contain all dogma and derivative doctrines.

Dogma is either 1) *de fide*, based upon divine revelation in Scripture or Tradition or maturation in the Church's understanding of divine revelation, or 2) *fides ecclesiastica*, a definitive, binding statement of faith made by an ecumenical council or when the pope speaks *ex-cathedra* (from the chair of Peter).[51] Purgatory is *fides ecclesiastica*. Purgatory was raised to the level of dogma in the late Middle Ages and has generated several doctrines—more on this in Chapter 7.

Theology is the study of God, his character, and how he acts in the cosmos, especially in his relationship with us. It is more speculative than dogma or doctrine but does not contradict either. It avoids *rationalism* (everything is knowable by reason) and *fideism* (faith alone is sufficient without learning about God).[52]

Dogma and doctrine are vital guides to help us better understand the metaphysical mystery of God's plan to reach us and to instruct our response to him in return. Together they help protect us from erroneous thinking and actions that lead us away from proper love of God, neighbor, and self and into sin.

3 – PURGATORY'S CALLING CARD

[T]here is a mysterious fact about the great words of our religious tradition: they cannot be replaced. All attempts to make substitutions ... have led to shallow and impotent talk. There are no substitutes for words like 'sin' and 'grace'.[53]
    Paul Tillich, Protestant Philosopher and Theologian

Without sin, there is no need for purgatory. As the Church is a "hospital" for sinners, purgatory heals the "sickness" in the soul remaining at death.[54] Sin impairs the spiritual health of the soul, dulls the conscience, harms the human psyche, and propagates ill effects in the world. Spiritual ill health impedes our union with God and others.

According to the Church, purgatory is not a required stopover between death and heaven for those in perfect spiritual health. A conversion in this life that proceeds from a fervent charity can attain the complete healing and purification of the sinner so that purgatory is unnecessary.[55] Such a conversion would align one's will perfectly with God's, just as Jesus's will was conformed perfectly to the Father.

Thus, purgatory is available for those who have died in God's friendship (*free from the guilt of unforgiven grave sin*) and have yet to remove all attachments to everything of higher priority than their love of God. Such attachments can include ourselves, others, and created goods—any "idol" that impairs our priorities and clouds the eyes of our soul.

If the measure of love is the person of Jesus Christ, all have fallen short in our love of God and others and proper self-love. (cf. Rom 3:23) So, while all have a conscience to discern right from wrong, good from evil, and an intellect capable of knowing God and absolute truth, we naturally tend toward moral wrongdoing and desire creatures and created goods over God. Our wills do not always will what God does, and we are disposed to moral wrongdoing.

We can no longer assume a common moral ground in the postmodern age. The Christian teaching on sin is buried deep within the graveyard of abandoned, out-of-date values. Sin has lost its sting as our consciences have been dulled and seared.

Popular culture rarely discusses sin, and when it does, as Hillary Brand observed, it is "frequently in ironic quotation marks and often used in terms of 'naughty but nice,' minor misdemeanors, something disapproved of, an outmoded Catholic shame culture, Islamic oppression or fundamentalist extremism. Rarely is it used in the way the Church understands it."[56] Not passing judgment on the sinner (a good thing) has been extrapolated to a blindness and denial of sin itself (a bad thing) and a particular intolerance for biblically-based Christian moral values.

Postmodernism misunderstands Jesus's message of mercy, characterizing it as a message of tolerance that denies sin and that no one needs to be forgiven. However, we must admit something is wrong, name our sins, and ask for forgiveness to receive God's healing mercy.[57]

Emergence of Sin

Catholicism teaches that all of God's creation is good, including human nature—although fallen—because God made us in his image and likeness.[58] (cf. Gen 1:26-28) While all admit to the presence of evil in the world, Christians believe that evil results from the sin of our first parents.[59]

In the third chapter of Genesis, we read that the incredible intimacy with God granted to our first parents was traded for a lesser good, resulting in the *first* sin. Even without a literal interpretation, Genesis 3 teaches that sin has serious and enduring consequences. With sin, a loss of innocence, guilt, shame, suffering, and death entered the world. You and I were born into a world already in chaos, our human nature weakened by our tendency to sin and to form unhealthy attachments to creatures and created goods. We follow in the missteps of our first parents.

This inherited tendency to sin is called *concupiscence*. The passing on of concupiscence is called *original sin*. In Catholic teaching, "original sin is the absence of original holiness and justice into which humans are born, distinct from the *actual sins* that a person commits."[60] Some effects of original sin include disordered sensual desires, a darkened intellect to discern truth, and a weakened will to choose good even when we know we should.

The Catholic Church teaches that Baptism removes all traces of the guilt of sin before God: original and actual sin (if the neophyte had attained the age of reason), but concupiscence remains.[61] Some Protestant faith traditions view Baptism as a symbolic act of obedience (modeling Christ's death and resurrection) or part of the conversion process (demonstrating one's commitment to follow Christ) rather than removing sin.

Guilt and Conscience

There is a difference between one's guilt before God and a guilty conscience. Guilt before God is an *objective* state caused by sin, thereby meriting eternal death rather than eternal union with God. (cf. Rom 6:23) God removes the guilt of our sin, counting us worthy of eternal life through the merits of Christ's redemption, our sincere repentance, and our reception of the Sacrament of Reconciliation. Human guilt or a guilty conscience is a *subjective* state when we judge ourselves as having compromised our standard of morality or ethics.

While human guilt is an unpleasant feeling, not all guilt is bad. Healthy guilt and unhealthy guilt are very different. With unhealthy guilt, we do not feel forgiven by God after sincerely confessing our sins, repenting, and making amends when possible. In extreme cases, unhealthy guilt can degenerate into scrupulosity. In healthy guilt, a rightly formed conscience appropriately sends a strong signal when we sin. Many jokes about "Catholic guilt" inappropriately equate unhealthy guilt with healthy guilt.

Healthy guilt is a gift of the Holy Spirit that we can nourish or quench. Within each person is the ability to know God, the source of all truth, beauty, and goodness. God equipped us with a conscience to help us differentiate good from evil, but we have a great tendency towards moral deception. Our judgment is clouded by our fallen nature and a world that has lost its moral compass and grasp of common truth. According to Philosopher J. Budziszewski, all really know right from wrong.[62]

Budziszewski distinguishes between three modes of conscience: cautionary (the teacher), accusatory (the judge), and avenging (the executioner). In cautionary mode, the conscience issues an avoidance and inhibitory warning; in accusatory mode, it indicts us for what we have done; and in avenging mode, it "punishes the soul who does wrong but who refuses to read the indictment."[63]

A spiritually healthy conscience is filled with remorse when we choose wrong. Budziszewski writes that the appropriate response for remorse is to flee from the wrong, confess it, admit what we have done, make atonement, pay the debt, and get back in right standing with ourselves, others, and God. But when we refuse to acknowledge our wrong, "the wrongdoer's life becomes more out of kilter"—we flee not from the wrong but attempt to suppress any thoughts about it. We grasp at a feeble restoration of lost intimacy "by seeking companions as guilty as ourselves ... we seek not to become just, but to justify ourselves."[64]

But what kind of healing is possible when we deny sin? There has been much misunderstanding regarding what the Church means by *freedom of conscience*. Freedom of conscience does not mean that we get to decide what is right or wrong as contrary to the Gospel or Catholic moral teachings found in the Catechism.[65] Sadly, postmodernism propels this misunderstanding and justifies "cherry-picking" among the Church's teachings on morality. The effect is a dulling of conscience and the removing of a sense of personal guilt for grave sin.

Venial and Mortal Sin

Human experience convinces us that some actions are inherently more evil than others. Just as our court system differentiates between types of crimes, most people would admit murder is worse (and deserves a worse penalty) than making an uncharitable comment during the heat of an argument. The spiritual analog in Catholic doctrine is that not all sin is of the same degree. Scripture specifies a distinction:

If you see your brother or sister committing what is not a mortal sin, you will ask, and God will give life to such a one—to those whose sin is not mortal. There is sin that is mortal; I do not say that you should pray about that. All wrongdoing is sin, but there is sin that is not mortal. (1 Jn 5:16-17)

Differentiating between sin that shuts a person off from eternal life (mortal sin), if not repented, and lesser sin (venial sin) has long been part of the Church's traditional teaching. The writings of St. Jerome (d. 420), St. Augustine (d. 430), St. Caesarius of Arles (d. 542-3), and St. Gregory the Great (d. 604) all embraced the distinction between mortal and venial sin.

St. Jerome differentiated between light and heavy offenses, citing 1 Jn 5:16-17. Jerome wrote that the "great difference between sins" impacted how their guilt before God was removed.[66] In the case of lesser sin, pardon and removal of guilt was achieved through prayer. However, prayer was insufficient for grave sin because removing guilt was "difficult" and required penance administered through the Church.[67]

St. Augustine referred to "venial sins which do not hinder the righteous man from the attainment of eternal life."[68] Echoing Jerome, he believed that venial sins may be washed away by prayer and almsgiving while other damnable sins [mortal sins] separate one from the Body of Christ.

Augustine's *Sermon to Catechumens on the Creed* outlines the early Christian theology on sin, how the guilt of sin is remitted, and the role of Baptism:

For those whom ye have seen doing [public] *penance,* [they] *have committed heinous things, either adulteries or some enormous crimes: for these they do penance. Because if theirs had been light sins, to blot out these, daily prayer would suffice. In three ways then are sins remitted in the Church; by Baptism, by prayer, by the greater humility of penance; yet God does not remit sins but to the baptized. The very sins which He remits first, He remits not but to the baptized. When? When they are baptized. The sins which are after remitted upon prayer, upon penance, to whom He remits, it is to the baptized that He remitteth.*[69]

A century later, Caesarius of Arles referred to lesser sins as petty or minor sins and to more serious sins as *criminal capitalia*,[70] which was the origin of capital sins popularized by Gregory the Great, destined to become a frequent theme in the art and literature of the

Middle Ages. Gregory identified "little and very small sins" such as "daily idle talk, immoderate laughter, negligence in the care of our family"[71] with those larger sins spawned by "pride, the queen of sins," surrendering the soul "immediately to seven principal vices, as its first progeny, ... vain glory, envy, anger, melancholy, avarice, gluttony, lust."[72]

Over time, this doctrine of mortal and venial sins acquired clear boundaries, especially through Aquinas's *Summa Theologica*. He wrote extensively on the difference between the two, stating that venial sin cannot become mortal, for it deserves only temporal punishment (discussed below). In contrast, a mortal sin deserves eternal punishment.[73] In the documents from the Ecumenical Councils of Florence during the 15th century and Trent in the 16th century, the term *mortal sin* is used in dogmatic statements.[74]

For a sin to be mortal, three conditions are required: grave matter, full knowledge of the gravity of the offense, and free consent of the will. In mortal sin, we become our own god, breaking off our friendship and communion with God and destroying our covenant with him. The *Catechism* states: "If mortal sin is not redeemed by repentance and God's forgiveness, it causes exclusion from Christ's kingdom and the eternal death of hell, for our freedom has the power to make choices for ever, with no turning back."[75]

In contrast, venial sin involves lesser matter, although it could involve grave matter should full knowledge or free consent be missing. Venial sin does not break off friendship with God nor deprive one of eternal life with God. However, venial sin predisposes one to more serious sin.

The usual route for the forgiveness of mortal sin is a valid reception of the Sacrament of Reconciliation (also called Penance or Confession)[76], which removes the *guilt* of sin and restores our right standing with God. We are, however, left to deal with the *temporal consequences* of our sins. So, while God can and does forgive the guilt of our sins (if we are truly repentant and have confessed our sins), the misery and suffering that our sins caused to ourselves and others remain.[77]

Most Protestants do not differentiate between mortal and venial sin, tending toward one of two implicit schools of theological thought: either all sin is mortal, or all sin is venial.[78] That all sin is mortal follows John Calvin's legalistic arguments that all sin is a rebellion against God and that the wages of sin are death. The other school argues that all sin is venial as we can do nothing to incur the loss of heaven once an act of faith has been made.

Eternal Versus Temporal Punishments

In Catholic teaching, sin has a double consequence: eternal and temporal punishment.[79] Christ paid in full the debt of the eternal punishment for our sins, but we are still left with the natural consequences of our sins to sort out. The wake of our sins rises high and far, impairing all our relationships with God, our neighbor, and ourselves. Sin adds to the suffering in the world.

But what exactly is *temporal punishment*? Temporal derives from *temporalis*, which means "of time." Punishment derives from *punire*, meaning "punish, correct, cause pain for some offense, or to take vengeance." Of those four meanings, the first three apply to temporal punishment, but the latter does not. God does not take vengeance; that is a human attribute. Temporal punishment "must not be conceived of as a kind of vengeance inflicted by God from without, but as following from the very nature of sin."[80]

Catholic convert and philosopher Neal Judisch summarizes well when he writes that temporal punishment "is not some additional 'judicial' penalty God imposes on sinners from on high with the expectation of their finding a way, somehow or other, to 'make satisfaction' in the form of 'payment' for their debts; it is ... the 'natural' punishment sin itself brings upon those who commit it."[81] Theologian and philosopher Romano Guardini, OSB (1858-1968), wrote that suffering is both the outcome of man's sin and its cure.[82]

Because God is perfectly holy, all sin offends him. He can and will forgive us if we ask him, but that doesn't fix the problem of the *sin within us*. For example, God's forgiveness does not automatically repair the breaks in our relationship with him and others. That problem is the temporal punishment of sin. We must take remedial action to excise the roots of our sinful brokenness to expiate our sin and regain spiritual health. Here, concrete examples help.

Suppose I lose my temper during a heated discussion and hurt a friend's feelings through my angry words. After a short while, I stop fuming and recognize that I have messed up. I am contrite, sincerely apologize to my friend, and ask if there is anything I can do to patch things up. Even if my friend accepts my apology, our relationship may feel strained. A temporal consequence of my sin is the change in our relationship resulting from the very nature of my sin. I may go to confession, fast, and pray for the restoration of the relationship, which goes a long way toward teaching me the horrific consequences of my lack of self-control over my tongue. Making amends is hard work, but the fruits of humility and self-control are always worth it.

Other sins, like the destruction of property, may require making amends or restitution as a matter of justice. What would we do if we discovered that our child had stolen something? We would need to teach the child that their action was wrong. We would want the child to be sorry and apologize. The child might be sorry that he got caught and apologize to get his parents off his back (imperfect contrition), but he could experience a profound change of heart, see that his actions were wrong, and be sorry for the harm done (perfect contrition). We would require that he return the item (if possible) or earn money to replace the item (if not). The child would likely lose some privileges. While contrition and a sincere apology are critical, justice demands reparation. "Sorry" wasn't quite enough to teach the child the seriousness of his action.

By analogy, we can understand temporal punishment best as loving discipline from a Father, simultaneously merciful and just, to nudge us toward spiritual rebirth.[83] Making a valid confession with sincere contrition may not remove all temporal punishment for our sins. The penance the priest assigns at the end of a good confession points the penitent toward healing but may not repair the harm and remove the suffering.

There may be additional work for personal rehabilitation and to make an expiation for the wake of our sin. Sometimes our sin leads to the sin in others. We may think our sin hurt no one but ourselves, but our brokenness, acted out in sin, casts its net of destruction.

The remission of sin is "only in the measure of the subjective dispositions of the penitent."[84] The *Catechism* points out that with the right attitude, patiently bearing suffering in this life and death itself, we can reduce our burden of the temporal punishment:

> *While patiently bearing sufferings and trials of all kinds and, when the day comes, serenely facing death, the Christian must strive to accept this temporal punishment of sin as a grace. He should strive by works of mercy and charity, as well as by prayer and the various practices of penance, to put off completely the "old man" and to put on the "new*

man."[85]

Like Catholics, Protestants believe that one's motives and behaviors may be transformed through suffering in this life: to put off the "old man" and put on the "new man." (cf. Eph 4:22-24) However, they would not accept that there is any suffering in the afterlife to complete the process of becoming the "new man."

Whether one is a Protestant who goes directly to God for the forgiveness of sin or a Catholic who first goes to God and then receives absolution through the Sacrament of Reconciliation to wipe away the guilt of sin, the consequences of sin are not immediately wiped out. Sin begets sin; each sin makes it easier to commit the same sin again. It is a great deal of work to rid oneself of the proclivity to sin.

In summary, the Church teaches that temporal punishment for sins can remain after death if not satisfied in this life through personal penance and a radical conversion in love. The valid reception of the Sacrament of Reconciliation has two effects: 1) *entirely removing the guilt* of our sins and 2) *partially removing the temporal punishment* due to sin, depending on the sin and the penitent's disposition.

Historical Development of Temporal Punishment

Initially, the early Church did not distinguish between the guilt and punishment due to sin and demanded long periods of penance for serious, post-baptismal sins. The Church recognized that sin impacted the individual sinner and the *entire* Christian community. For that reason, absolution and reconciliation remained part of the *public* liturgy. Public confession was "strongly endorsed throughout the first six centuries" and was sometimes the only option.[86] While there were some "variations in its practice, public confession was universally required for a trilogy of major sins: apostasy, murder, and adultery."[87]

The penitent's prayers were joined to the prayer of the Church body and the intercessory prayer of the priest.[88] The penitent wasn't allowed to fully participate in worship or receive the Eucharist until he completed his penance, which could take years.[89]

When the Church's penitential practices evolved from public to private confession, the guilt of sin before God became separate from its temporal punishment. Once the penitent received ecclesial absolution of his sins in private auricular confession, he could fully rejoin the worship community. Thus, the guilt of his sin was removed before the completion of the penance. The ecclesial penance became associated with the temporal punishment due to the penitent's sins. This distinction occurred without any relaxation of the actual penances or a sense of anything new happening.[90] By the 10th century, the Sacrament of Reconciliation assumed the basic form we would recognize today.[91]

In writing on the effect of contrition, Aquinas fully articulated the separation of guilt of sin before God and the temporal punishment due to sin.[92] In his *Summa Theologica*, Aquinas mentions the temporal punishment of sin fifty-seven times. The context includes differentiating the eternal punishment due to mortal sins from the temporal punishment due to venial sins, ecclesial penances, and purgatory.

In Catholicism, temporal punishment for sin can teach us lessons in this life or in the afterlife. Lessons learned earlier (in this life) bear the joyful fruit of reconciliation with God and others and reduce the "workload" in purgatory later—the topic of Chapter 6. The next chapter examines the theological basis for accepting or rejecting temporal punishment due to sin in the afterlife and the need to complete unlearned lessons in love or, equivalently, the need for purgatory.

4 – JUSTIFICATION & SANCTIFICATION

What actually saves us is the full ascent of faith. But in most of us, that basic option is buried under a great deal of wood, hay and straw. Only with difficulty can it peer out from behind the latticework of an egoism we are powerless to pull down with our own hands. Man is the recipient of divine mercy, yet this does not exonerate him from the need to be transformed. [93]

Joseph Ratzinger (Pope Benedict XVI)

All Christians agree that through the redeeming death and resurrection of Jesus Christ, God offers us the free gift of salvation. All Christians agree that our souls are immortal, and we will ultimately spend eternity in heaven or hell. Those who end up in heaven are saved; those in hell are lost. All Christians agree that in heaven, there is *no trace of sin.* (cf. Heb 12:14)

But purgatory is challenging to discuss with any broad Christian audience. Various Christian faith traditions understand the related conceptual issues differently: the transformation of the self between death and heavenly glory, our communion with the dead, prayers for the dead, and indulgences.[94]

The theological controversy surrounding purgatory hinges on the doctrine of *salvation*: how the merits of Christ's life, passion, death, and resurrection redeem and save believers and how these merits of Christ are granted to us. In this chapter, we discover that different theological treatments of *justification* and *sanctification* (to be defined) separate Catholicism's embrace of purgatory from Protestantism's denouncement. For Catholics, purgatory is an intermediate state for souls not sufficiently purified for heaven with a remaining debt of temporal punishment.[95] For most Protestants, purgatory is theologically unnecessary and an insult to the sufficiency of Christ's redeeming work.

Theological Differences Impacting Acceptance of Purgatory

The crux of the disagreement arises when we speak of *individual* salvation, justification, and sanctification. So, while Christians can generally agree, the "devil" is in the details, or as John Calvin (1509-1564) wrote, "[P]urgatory is a pernicious fiction of Satan, that it makes void the cross of Christ, … [and] intolerably insults the Divine mercy, and weakens and overturns our faith."[96]

Below are high-level, working definitions of salvation, justification, and sanctification that most, if not all, Christians would accept:

- *Salvation* is the assurance of life eternal with God.
- *Justification* is the achievement of right standing before God.
- *Sanctification* is the requisite holiness to enter heaven and commune with God.

Traditional Protestant theology holds that "the possession of saving faith is a *sufficient* condition for enjoying eternal union and fellowship with God in heaven (emphasis added)."[97] In other words, a person's faith alone sufficiently justifies them, assuring them of their salvation. Thus, salvation is viewed primarily as *justification, independent of sanctification.*

The details that comprise saving faith vary across Protestant denominations. But for most, Christ imputes his sanctification immediately before or at the moment of death for those with saving faith. This imputation is called *forensic (or legal) justification*, whereby a "divine verdict of acquittal [is] pronounced on the believing sinner [declaring him] … 'not guilty' [of his sins] because *Christ has taken his place*, living a perfect life according to God's law and suffering for his sins (emphasis added)."[98]

In Catholicism, justification is both an *event*, including the Sacrament of Baptism, and a *process* where the will and intellect cooperate with divine grace to achieve regeneration in Christ.

Excerpts from the *Catechism* flesh out these two aspects:

- *The grace of the Holy Spirit has the power to justify us, that is, to cleanse us from our sins and to communicate to us 'the righteousness of God through faith in Jesus Christ' and through Baptism[.]*
- *The first work of the grace of the Holy Spirit is conversion, effecting justification[.]*[99]
- *Justification detaches man from sin ... and purifies his heart of sin. ... It reconciles man with God. It frees from the enslavement to sin, and it heals.*[100]
- *Justification establishes cooperation between God's grace and man's freedom. On man's part it is expressed by the assent of faith to the Word of God, which invites him to conversion, and in the cooperation of charity with the prompting of the Holy Spirit who precedes and preserves his assent.*[101]

Catholicism espouses *infused justification* as opposed to *forensic justification*. The source of infused justification remains Christ, but the individual is responsible for cooperating with God's grace to transform their lives. This *cooperation with grace* assumes some action on man's part to achieve the requisite sanctification.

In summary, Catholics believe Christ did the work to complete our justification. However, our sanctification is completed in cooperation with him through the action of the Holy Spirit and sacramental channels of grace.[102] Thus, Catholics believe that sanctification or growth in holiness is a *process subsequent to justification*.[103] There is a synergism between God's grace and man's free will response to that grace in Catholic teaching.

Therein lies the rub. Protestant theology asserts justification needs no separate process of sanctification since forensic justification assumes Christ's perfect holiness will be imputed to the believer at death. The Catholic position does not diminish the work of Christ but emphasizes the cooperation of the human will with God's grace to bring about sanctification.

The reader may be surprised that this sounds nothing like the traditional Protestant definition of Catholic justification, i.e., that Catholics believe that good works save them. To understand where the charge of good works comes from, we turn to the contrasting concept: *divine monergism* and the process of sanctification.

Divine monergism holds that God works through the Holy Spirit to justify the individual *without* his explicit cooperation.[104] One can think of this as imputed righteousness, a concept born with Martin Luther and amplified by John Calvin.

Protestant faith traditions that hold to divine monergism include Lutheran, Reformed traditions, Southern Baptist, Pentecostal, Assembly of God, Presbyterian, and Evangelical. Methodists believe justification is an event (accepting Jesus as Lord and Savior) but recognize that the individual must cooperate with grace.

Decision theology and *permanence theology* often go hand in hand with divine monergism. Decision theology is the belief that a personal decision to accept Jesus as one's Lord and Savior seals the deal for one's salvation. Permanence theology asserts that one cannot lose their salvation or, equivalently, "once saved, always saved." Protestant Reformed denominations, including Presbyterians and some Baptist denominations, ascribe to permanence, while Lutherans, Orthodox Christians, Pentecostals, and Methodists don't. Catholicism rejects both decision theology and permanence theology.

Closest to Catholicism's teaching on justification is the Orthodox Christian view, where justification (or Theosis) is an event that includes Baptism but is a process demonstrated by righteous living.[105]

Protestant philosopher Jerry Walls wrote that it "was a Protestant innovation to separate justification from sanctification and to construe [justification] primarily in legal and forensic terms."[106] Forensic justification does not require a changed inward character of a sinner; instead, it is a divine declarative act announcing and determining a person's relationship to the law and justice of God. In other words, a person's character is *covered over* by Christ's atonement.

So, while all Christians agree that 1) nothing impure can enter heaven, and 2) few people are fully purified (or sanctified) at death, they disagree on how that morally sanctified nature comes about.

Traditional Protestant theology maintains that the justified believer wears God's righteousness, imputed at death or immediately thereafter. In a loose sense, when God the Father looks at the justified believer, he sees his Son, Jesus. Thus, the most common Protestant theology of *justification* does not require any atoning work or purification after death before heaven.

Catholic theology asserts that the believer is engaged in a period of renewal and sanctification that begins in this life, and, for some, that process extends beyond the grave through the mystery of an intermediate state called purgatory. Thus, Catholics adhere to a theology of *sanctification* after death for those who depart this life in God's friendship but are still imperfect. This postmortem process is the essence of purgatory. While on this side of the grave, Catholics work out their salvation in fear and trembling with a torrent of graces from the Holy Spirit, including (but not limited to) the reception of the sacraments.

Steps Towards an Ecumenical Understanding of Justification

How one is justified and sanctified is at the theological root of the rejection of purgatory by Protestants.[107] But differences in justification have sown a wide field of divisiveness. Philosopher J. Budziszewski recounts that the theological difference of justification was behind the claim of his "old Baptist teachers that Catholicism was not Christian."[108] Philosopher and Catholic convert Robert Koons wrote that much hinged on the issue of justification, and if the Catholic Church had this wrong, then "her claim to apostolic authority" was untenable, but if correct, then the Reformation and its break in Christian unity were "built on a mistake."[109]

Given the theological differences between justification and sanctification, it is easy to see how tension can exist between devout Catholics and staunch Protestants. Protestants who believe they are saved by faith alone believe Catholics think they are waved into heaven by their good works. Philosopher Peter Kreeft, reflecting on his path from Dutch Calvinism to Catholicism, wrote that what he had once labeled as Catholic "work righteousness" instead of "salvation by faith alone" turned out to be "works of love," the "other half of faith."[110]

Understanding the differences and the commonalities between what Protestants and Catholics mean by salvation, justification, and sanctification can have a profound ecumenical effect on Christian unity.

In 1999, the Lutheran World Federation and the Roman Catholic Church signed the Joint Declaration on the Doctrine of Justification (JDDJ) after years of work.[111] This historic document stated that the 16th-century mutual denouncements between the Council of Trent and the Lutheran Confessions were no longer in effect regarding justification.[112] Each understood the other's way of thinking and was willing to tolerate the other's differences, resolving one of the issues of the Protestant Reformation, stating that "the Lutheran and the Catholic explications of justification are in their difference open to one another and do not destroy the consensus regarding the basic truths."[113]

Remaining differences were still acknowledged, primarily in areas that spilled over into sanctification and assurance of salvation, specifically the Catholic teaching that a) by man's free will, he must freely cooperate with the grace of justification and can refuse God's grace and that b) man is responsible for his actions, good or bad.

Later, other Protestant denominations signed the JDDJ: in 2006, the World Methodist Council; in 2016, the Anglican Consultative Council; in 2017, the World Communion of Reformed Churches.

J. Budziszewski wrote of the impact that the 1999 JDDJ had on his faith journey. "At the time, when I was still firmly Protestant, it [JDDJ] had struck me like a thunderclap. Recalling Luther's words that justification was the article on which the [Catholic] Church stands or falls, I thought as I read it, 'The Reformation is over.'"[114] With nothing more to protest, Budziszewski entered the Catholic Church after years of intellectual wrangling with himself about whether he should convert.

5 – MODELS OF PURGATORY

Our souls demand Purgatory, don't they? Would it not break the heart if God said to us, 'It is true, my son, that your breath smells and your rags drip with mud and slime, but we are charitable here and no one will upbraid you with these things, nor draw away from you. Enter into the joy?' Should we not reply, 'With submission, sir, and if there is no objection, I'd rather be cleaned first.' 'It may hurt, you know'— 'Even so, sir.'[115]
C. S. Lewis

In the Old Testament, strict ritualistic laws taught the Israelites about the purity and perfection of God. In the New Testament, Jesus exhorted his disciples to be perfect (cf. Mt 5:48) and holy (cf. 1 Pt 1:16) just as their heavenly Father is perfect. Entering heaven and communing with God requires our moral perfection and untainted holiness. Catholics and Protestants disagree on how we achieve the requisite transformation. We have seen that disagreement results from differing meanings ascribed to *justification* and *sanctification*.

The Protestant position of *forensic justification* requires that God instantly sanctifies the individual at death. But we must ask: if God could zap us into perfect holiness at our death, why would he not do so now and save the world (and us) from much suffering? If God will clean us up perfectly without our cooperation, why wait?

The Catholic position of *infused justification* holds that personal sanctification is the joint work of God's grace and the individual's response to that grace. Infused justification is philosophically and theologically consistent with sanctification beginning on earth and continuing after death if necessary. What are the implications for the individual, still clinging to his sins at death and lacking maturity in love? The answer of the Roman Catholic Church is purgatory.

In this chapter, we explore the nature of this purgatory by

considering several theoretical models based on the Catholic doctrines of 1) temporal punishment due to sin and 2) infused justification.

A *debt of temporal punishment*—not fully discharged before death—suggests a first model. This model emphasizes divine *judgment*, characterized by *satisfaction* or enduring the *punishment* for our sins. Here, the individual must pay "to the last penny" the remaining temporal penalties in the accounting of his sins.

In contrast, the *unfinished work of infused justification*—the purification of man's sinful heart and detachment from sin—suggests a second. This second model emphasizes divine *mercy* and *sanctification* to ready us for the beatific vision.[116]

Which view is correct? Are they mutually exclusive? Can God's mercy and justice act independently of each other?

Divine Mercy and Divine Justice

If we look to the crucified and risen Christ, we glimpse the mysterious and proper relationship between divine justice and divine mercy. Through *mercy*, God the Father offers his Son for our salvation. In *justice*, Jesus offers himself back to the Father. The two reciprocal "actions" in one God open up for humanity the grace for our eternal salvation. This offering of the Son to the Father did not minimize sin or its consequences. Yet, God's justice, in requiring the perfect sacrifice, did not act without his mercy for us.

> *Both these things—justice and grace—must be seen in their correct inner relationship. Grace does not cancel out justice. It does not make wrong into right. It is not a sponge which wipes everything away, so that whatever someone has done on earth ends up being of equal value.* [117]

The Catholic theology of purgatory embodies the mystery of how God simultaneously acts with justice and mercy. This insight renders purgatory crucial to our hope and helps mitigate anxiety about what comes after death. Philosopher Peter Kreeft struggled with the dogma of purgatory until he realized that we can no more escape God's justice than we can his mercy.[118]

We like to parse God into his attributes because that is how we understand things: piecemeal. We desire to separate God's mercy from his justice as if those divine attributes operated independently.

In us, they certainly can and most often do. But when it comes to purgatory, they are indivisible.

Catholic philosopher Josef Pieper (1904-1997) wrote that the theological virtue of hope removes the apparent antithesis between divine justice and divine mercy. "Only hope is able to comprehend the reality of God that surpasses all antithesis, to know that his mercy is identical with his justice and his justice with his mercy."[119] Pieper warned against *despair*, which focuses solely on divine justice, and *presumption*, which focuses exclusively on divine mercy.[120]

Hans Urs von Balthasar (1905-1988), a Catholic priest and theologian, recognized this human tendency to separate divine justice from divine mercy, quoting a sermon of St. Augustine:

> *"Do not imagine that these two [mercy and justice] can be separate in God in any way. They may at first seem to be mutually opposed, so that whoever is merciful would not uphold justice and whoever adheres unconditionally to justice would forget about mercy. But God is omnipotent: he neither lets go of justice in showing mercy nor of mercy in judging justly."*[121]

Pope Benedict XVI understood justice as a "catalyst for purification, not something operating opposed or mutually exclusive to it."[122] In *Spe Salvi*, he wrote that God's judgment can give us hope specifically because it is both grace [mercy] and justice. "If it were merely grace, making all earthly things cease to matter, God would still owe us an answer to the question about justice—the crucial question that we ask of history and of God. If it were merely justice, in the end, it could bring only fear to us as well."[123]

Two Theoretical Models—or One?

For the moment, however, assume that it is possible to separate God's justice and mercy and place these divine attributes at opposite ends of a continuum. Assign a model of purgatory at each endpoint.

On the extreme end of mercy, purgatory becomes a state solely of purification (sanctification) and healing. Here, a loving God cleanses and rehabilitates the soul. Over time, the brokenness and residue of sin still clinging to the soul at the end of one's earthly life is removed, and the soul is healed. Any lack of virtue keeping the soul from the object of its passionate love—God—is matured. This is the *Sanctification Model* of purgatory.

The Sanctification Model does not rule out some suffering, much like a parent telling a child they must apologize for uncharitable words or actions. This parental action is not to punish the child but to engender virtue.

At the opposite end of the continuum, the *Satisfaction Model* characterizes purgatory as a state of punishment demanded by God's justice. Here, the individual makes satisfaction and expiation for his sins, working off the temporal punishment not fully discharged by penance or expiation while on earth. Through purgatorial suffering, divine justice exacts full payment for every unfair, unkind, unforgiving, uncharitable, selfish, deceitful, or impure thought, word, and action of our past life that has not entirely destroyed our love of God.[124]

At the center of the continuum is a model of purgatory that serves dual purposes: purification (sanctification) and punishment (satisfaction). Let's call this the *Unified Model*. Here, purgatory is demanded by God's justice and equally a gift of his mercy. The two elements of satisfaction and sanctification are not distinct or unrelated. Such is the Catholic theology of purgatory, as argued by philosopher Neal Judisch, who maintains that the two views are one and the same when understood properly.[125]

Judisch is not the first to argue that point. In 1855, F. W. Faber, D.D., a convert from Anglicanism to Catholicism under the tutelage of John Henry Newman, wrote that there "have always been two views of purgatory prevailing in the Church, not contradictory the one of the other, but rather expressive of the mind and devotion of those who have embraced them."[126] Faber characterized the spirit of one view "as a holy fear of offending God, a desire for bodily austerities, a great value put upon indulgences, an extreme horror of sin, and a habitual trembling before the judgments of God."[127] He characterized the second view as focusing "on the worship of God's purity and sanctity," the soul sense of self "from God's point of view," and merging "its own interests in His [God's]."[128] We recognize these two views as the Satisfaction and Sanctification Models, respectively.

In the main body of his *Summa Theologica*, Aquinas mentions purgatory in the context of mortal and venial sin, temporal punishment, penance, indulgences, and the afterlife. But purgatory is extensively treated in two appendices written by his students after his death, summarizing their teacher's views.[129] His writings favor a Unified Model "with the accent falling on satisfaction."[130] For Aquinas, there is no tension between the sanctification and satisfaction components of purgatory; both are necessarily unified, as penance has no transforming, purifying power unless freely embraced.

Baltimore Catechism's Model of Purgatory

The *Baltimore Catechism*, first published in 1885, was the standard text used in Catholic schools in the United States until the late 1960s.[131] As a child, I remember well the question-and-answer format from my religion classes.[132] The catechisms were numbered; the higher the number, the greater the detail, targeting progressively older students to prepare them for First Communion, Confirmation, and post-Confirmation study.

The authors of the original *Baltimore Catechism* are unknown but worked as representatives of the Third Plenary Council of Baltimore.[133] The 1921 edition contained supplemental guides written by Rev. Thomas L. Kinkead but was otherwise unchanged from the 1885 Catechism.[134]

The *Baltimore Catechism* presents elements of the Satisfaction and Sanctification Models. The questions and answers below are from the section "On the Last Judgment and the Resurrection, Hell, Purgatory, and Heaven."[135]

> *Q. 1381. What is Purgatory?*
> *A. Purgatory is the state in which those suffer for a time who die guilty of venial sins, or without having* satisfied *for the* punishment *due to their sins* (emphasis added).
>
> *Q. 1382. Why is this state called Purgatory?*
> *A. This state is called Purgatory because in it the souls are* purged or purified *from all their stains; and it is not, therefore, a permanent or lasting state for the soul* (emphasis added).
>
> *Q. 1383. Are the souls in Purgatory sure of their salvation?*
> *A. The souls in Purgatory are sure of their salvation, and they will enter heaven as soon as they are completely* purified *and made worthy to enjoy that presence of God which is called the Beatific Vision* (emphasis

added).

Q. 1386. Since God loves the souls in Purgatory, why does He punish them?

A. Though God loves the souls in Purgatory, He punishes *them because His holiness requires that nothing defiled may enter heaven and His* justice *requires that everyone be* punished *or rewarded according to what he deserves* (emphasis added).

In 1949, the Confraternity of Christian Doctrine (CCD) published the *Revised Confraternity Catechism*, which significantly reorganized the original material from the previous editions with only minor edits to the original content. To address pedagogical criticisms from earlier editions, the CCD added pictures, definitions, doctrinal summaries, scriptural support, classroom discussion aids, a detailed section on the Mass, and prayers.

The *Revised Confraternity Catechism* states that if the soul at death "is in venial sin or is still burdened by a debt of temporal punishment, it will go to purgatory until full *satisfaction* is made and it is made worthy of the presence of God. ... God *punishes* these souls, not in a spirit of vengeance, but because He loves them and wills that they be fully *purified* so that they can be admitted to His presence (emphasis added)."[136]

Punishment (satisfaction for sins) and purification (sanctification needed for heaven) are always present in all three versions of the *Baltimore Catechism* but with an emphasis on the Satisfaction Model. There is no mention of God's mercy, only his justice, in conjunction with purgatory.

Vatican II (1962-1965) brought many changes to the Catholic Church, including its approach to teaching the truths of the Catholic faith. The transition had a few bumps when the CCD pulled its catechism in the late 1960s without a replacement. My religious education went from a black-and-white *Baltimore Catechism* experience to a fuzzy kumbaya-like encounter. However, my understanding of purgatory remained firmly parked in the "garage" of the Satisfaction Model, perhaps because it was never mentioned in school again. Ever.

The *Baltimore Catechism* is important because, for many practicing and non-practicing Catholics of my generation, their understanding of purgatory has never matured to the more hopeful theological expression transmitted in the new *Catechism of the Catholic Church*.

The Model for a New Century

In response to a growing crisis in catechesis after Vatican II, Pope John Paul II commissioned a new catechism in 1986. Joseph Cardinal Ratzinger (later Pope Benedict XVI) led the commission.

In 1992, Pope John Paul II presented the world with the new *Catechism of the Catholic Church* to shine "the light of faith" into "situations and problems which had not yet emerged in the past."[137] A polished second edition followed shortly thereafter and, in 2000, was published in English.[138] Due to a much wider readership of laypersons, extending beyond the targeted audience of bishops, the *Catechism of the Catholic Church* became an international best-seller.

The section on purgatory is entitled "The Final Purification, or Purgatory," consisting of only 378 words.[139] This section represents about one page out of the approximately 900 pages in the voluminous *Catechism*—not much.

One might wonder if the Church has now adopted a Sanctification Model for purgatory after reading the first paragraph (§1030), which sounds like a Purification Model of purgatory:

All who die in God's grace and friendship, but still imperfectly purified, are indeed assured of their eternal salvation; but after death they undergo purification, so as to achieve the holiness necessary to enter the joy of heaven.

In the following paragraph (§1031), no mention of the expiation of sin or satisfying an unpaid debt of temporal punishment is made. Punishment is referenced, but only to distance it from the punishment of hell. The last sentence references fire but in a historical and cleansing context:

The Church gives the name Purgatory to this final purification of the elect, which is entirely different from the punishment of the damned ... The tradition of the Church, by reference to certain texts of Scripture, speaks of a cleansing fire.

The third paragraph (§1032) connects the doctrine of purgatory with Scripture, prayer for the dead, and the ability of the living to help those in purgatory through penitential exercises.[140] How these exercises help the dead is not clarified.

This teaching is also based on the practice of prayer for the dead, already mentioned in Sacred Scripture ... The Church also commends almsgiving, indulgences, and works of penance undertaken on behalf of the dead[.]

Accepting a philosophical or theological position that purgatory exists does not logically require the concomitant position that the living can help or offer relief to the dead through suffrages. In other words, belief in the efficacy of prayers for the dead is sufficient but not necessary for belief in some intermediate state, such as purgatory, to make sense. To be clear, however, the Catholic Church affirms both.

The connection between purgatory and temporal punishment due to sin is in the *Catechism of the Catholic Church*. However, one must do some digging. The relationship between temporal punishment and purgatory is located within the articles on the Sacrament of Reconciliation within the section on "Indulgences"[141] rather than in the section "The Final Purification, or Purgatory." The Church has bound indulgences tightly to her teaching on purgatory.[142] (Indulgences, while not a required Catholic practice, are dogmatically confirmed by the Church for souls in purgatory.)

Religious philosopher Jerry Walls noticed a shift in the *Catechism's* description of purgatory from earlier doctrinal statements that he described as an ambiguous combination of Sanctification and Satisfaction Models. With the new *Catechism's* treatment of purgatory, Walls concluded that sanctification was the "primary if not the sole emphasis" in the formal doctrinal statements of the Catholic Church.[143] Although sympathetic to Walls's conclusion, I believe there was no change in doctrinal statements, only a shift in emphasis per the stated goal for the new *Catechism*—to respond "in a new way ... to the questions of our age" rather than to rewrite the Church's dogmatic teachings.[144]

Philosopher Neal Judisch, a Catholic convert from Reformed Presbyterianism, presents a cogent synthesis of Catholic teaching on purgatory from both philosophical and theological viewpoints. He concludes that the Satisfaction Model (which most, if not all, Protestants reject outright) and the Sanctification Model (which some Protestants are open to) are the same (a Unified Model, my terminology) when appropriately understood. An excerpt follows.

> *[T]he exclusive object of purgatory according to the Satisfaction Model is to allow those who die in the love of God to suffer the 'temporal punishments' and 'make satisfaction' for sins, where this ... is strictly equated with the process whereby the forgiven-but-lapsable*[145] *individual is purified of his disposition to sin and made inherently holy. ... In other*

words: the Satisfaction Model is equivalent to the Sanctification Model.[146]

Judisch is particularly sensitive to the Protestant and Catholic understanding of justification (saving faith). In the next chapter, we shall see that other Protestant philosophers and theologians, while not fully accepting the Catholic idea of cooperating with grace in the "process" of justification, see a need for a sanctification role for a postmortem purgation.

There is no binding Catholic doctrine on the "spatial or temporal character of purgatory, on how many Christians go through purgatory, or on the intensity or extent of their sufferings."[147] While there have been times when popular opinion seemed to indicate otherwise. Church *dogma* and *doctrine* have always been silent on those matters.

The Church has written sparingly in her dogmatic proclamations regarding purgatory through the Council of Florence in the 15th century, the Council of Trent a hundred years later, and in the *Catechism of the Catholic Church*.

6 – THE "WORK" OF PURGATORY

Can we not formulate this teaching in a way that, on the one hand, completely accords with the Church's older doctrinal statements and with Rome's exhortations at the present time and yet, on the other hand, permits us to see in this formulation something that seems "realizable," intelligent, credible and compatible with the rest of our anthropology? [148]

Karl Rahner S.J.

In purgatory, we complete the "work" of our sanctification, started in this life, to be wholly remade into Christ's image and readied for heaven without the hindrance of past sins and their attendant spiritual blindness. Thus, purgatory becomes "the inwardly necessary process of transformation in which a person becomes capable of Christ, capable of God, and thus capable of [unfettered] unity with the whole communion of saints."[149]

In this chapter, we contemplate the nature of this "work," constrained by the requirement that our sense of self *remains intact* in the afterlife. Thus, we enter the realm of *theology*: man's attempt to understand God's mystery and revelation.

Theology is far more speculative than dogma or doctrine, pursuing "investigations beyond dogma, having dogma always for its guide" to throw "light on what is obscure in the definitions; to make precise what they leave vague; sometimes, to guess at the implications of their silence."[150]

The Catholic Church teaches that the human will is fixed at death. Thus, purgatory is not a chance to do life all over again and choose differently. How we have lived and loved opens us up to respond to Absolute Truth or closes us down entirely. At our particular judgment, we will see ourselves "without a shadow of protection" and "without pride, vanity, evasion, or indifference."[151] Our choices in this life (i.e., whether we died as God's friend or, equivalently, in a state of grace) condition our response to the truth revealed about ourselves.

Purgatory is a chance to reform our "thinking" to become perfectly aligned with the mind of Christ if we are open to it. Not all will be, for the soul must humble itself completely. The soul must admit and own its sins—the offense of its sins to God, the damage caused to others, and the harm to itself. Will we "see" purgatory as the gift it is and willingly submit to its painful lessons? The soul must "complete the lessons" in purgatory it has failed to learn while on earth. These "lessons" may be viewed as completing the temporal punishment due to sin. The soul's eagerness to give itself over to these lessons—no matter how painful—is facilitated by meeting Christ and seeing its earthly life through the eyes of Absolute Truth. Without this sanctification or rehabilitation, a barrier exists to our union with God and others in heaven.

Purgatory is not a second chance to be saved for those who die with *no* flicker of love in their souls and their will wholly turned away from God. But how could a soul turn away from God when it meets Christ "face to face"? Pride, unforgiveness, and hatred oppose the requisite humility to be a willing and eager "student" in purgatory.

Hardness of heart freezes out the humility to admit wrongdoing. It spawns a prideful refusal to say, "I'm sorry," denies ownership of past wrongs, and extinguishes a desire to make things right. The hard-hearted soul has become its own measure of absolute truth—its own god. For him, the prison of unforgiveness is preferable to the "work" of purgatory. Such a soul has no appetite for rehabilitation, refuses sanctification, and chooses hell.

God is concerned with true repentance, a turning of the heart and will toward Him and away from that which separates us from Him and impairs our ability to *love*. God is the perfect communion of love and unity in his trinitarian nature: Father, Son, and Holy Spirit. The trinitarian aspect of love teaches us that love is essentially relational. If purgatory aims to complete our sanctification and perfection in love, we must ask, "What is love, and how do we become perfected in love in purgatory?"

Perfection in Love

Aquinas defined the fullness of love as willing the good of the beloved and the desire for union with the beloved.[152] Thomist philosopher Eleonore Stump writes that these two desires are interconnected and that, ultimately, human love is directed towards union with God and is shareable in union with others.[153] Thus, "a compromised relation to God exhibits itself in compromised relations to oneself and others alike."[154] Those compromised relations are the destructive harvest of sin.

Love that seeks the good of the other, even to the sacrifice of self-interest, requires deepening the psychologically and spiritually healthy love of self. Judisch, "leaning" upon insights from Aquinas and Stump, explains it this way:

> [S]anctification by its nature involves psychic integration around or as directed upon the [ultimate] good, which in turn entails wholeheartedly wanting the good for oneself. And if internal disorders—if conflicts of the mind and the will relative to the good—impede sanctification, then transcending these internal divisions results in sanctification and in self-unity both. But to desire the good for a person and to desire union with that person is to love that person. Therefore, sanctification entails self-love. These insights suggest a way of understanding the dynamics of pain, shame, and regret as features of temporal punishment in Purgatory.[155]

Certainly, then, part of purgatory's work is to remove obstacles to proper love of self, others, and God. Depending on the state of the soul, it could experience excruciating pain, finally accepting the truths that the soul spent a lifetime running from or denying—especially about itself.

Romano Guardini (1885-1968), a Catholic priest, philosopher, and theologian, has provided a powerful reflection. He theorizes that the whole nature of man is "plunged into recreating grace, through the mystery of effectual repentance, comes out new-made."[156]

Guardini intimates that at death, in the presence of Christ, everything is revealed about our life—the good and the bad of what we have done or have failed to do. By grace, we have a share in Christ's righteousness, but it does not cover our imperfections like a cloak. While God's love and forgiveness remake us with a new heart and a new eternal life, it does not change what we have done. That requires "change, purification, and reparation."[157]

God's grace brings about renewal "but not by a method that simply cancels all that we did on earth, [such as] the weaknesses in the structure [and foundation] of our life, the faults, the blindness" and, although still present, [in our soul, these spiritual deficits] are brought into the light of God's truth."[158] Everything of our past life is brought under the action of this truth and is redeemed. How is this done? According to Guardini, the pain of seeing ourselves as God sees us "is inconceivable, but it is effective."[159]

The "pain that was refused [on earth] must [in purgatory] be accepted; the truth that has escaped cognition must be learned; the imperfect love must be made full and perfect."[160] It is not that the soul will substitute a new version of its past, but the "contrite man returns to the past act and enters into it until he knows and judges it with his reason, his wills, his intentions, and does so in the presence of the living, holy God," but in some mysterious way "evil, by being lived again, is made over into good."[161]

Catholic theologian John Thiel, in seeming agreement with Guardini, proposes that being a "disciple of Jesus means that, even in the afterlife, the bonds of reconciliation that unite the communion of the saints must be forged in the work of forgiveness, made and remade in acts of love that grace those who forgive as much as those who are forgiven."[162]

Guardini and Thiel's reflections counter medieval theology, where "suffering souls are utterly *passive* with respect to their own remediation where they can do nothing to improve their condition, diminish their suffering, or shorten their time of purgation (emphasis added)."[163]

According to theologian Karl Rahner, S.J., Church dogma does not require us to think of purgatory "as a purely passive endurance of vindictive punishments" that once endured would "release one in exactly the same condition in which he commenced this state of purification." Rahner saw compelling reasons to think of purgatory as a gradual maturing process, where "all the powers of the human being become slowly integrated into the basic decision of the free person."[164]

John Paul II analogized the temporal punishment of purgatory as a "medicine," encouraging the sinner to undertake his profound journey of conversion towards the fullness of love.[165] This conversion has the same purpose as fasting, almsgiving, self-mortification, and ecclesial penances assigned in the Sacrament of Reconciliation.

Hans Urs von Balthasar, S.J., describes purgatory as "'the terrible torture of having to settle now all the things we have dreaded our whole life long. The doors we have frantically held shut are now torn open.'"[166] Stripped of our blinders, we can become all God intended us to be for the first time. Balthazar compared the purgatorial fire to the sinner's encounter with Christ's eyes. This theme of purgatorial fire as Christ himself reemerges eloquently in Pope Benedict XVI's encyclical *Spe Salvi*:

> *His gaze, the touch of his heart heals us through an undeniably painful transformation 'as through fire.' But it is a blessed pain, in which the holy power of his love sears through us like a flame, enabling us to become totally ourselves and thus totally of God. ... In this way the inter-relation between justice and grace also becomes clear: the way we live our lives is not immaterial, but our defilement does not stain us forever if we have at least continued to reach out towards Christ, towards truth and towards love. Indeed, it has already been burned away through Christ's Passion. At the moment of judgment, we experience and we absorb the overwhelming power of his love over all the evil in the world and in ourselves. The pain of love becomes our salvation and our joy.*[167]

The unifying thread of the above theological thoughts is that purgatory is the state whereby we perfect ourselves in love. The soul actively pursues this work, having received final clarity of vision into its earthly life's good and spoilt fruit. The soul undertakes this "work" of justice—voluntarily, actively, and painfully—but with complete confidence and, therefore, joy that through the provision of divine mercy, God provides the medicine to purify our love.

The soul's desire for union with God becomes overpowering, yet its remaining stain of imperfections separates it from the very love that consumes and inflames it. To the extent that the soul has made amends and reformed its heart from its past failures to love God, our neighbors, and itself, those sins do not separate the soul from its union with God. But the remaining stains drive the soul to throw itself into the purifying "fire" of God's Love and voluntarily enter the state of purification and reparation.

Christian Anthropology, Human Experience, and Continuity of Self

From the Christian standpoint, a human being is matter [body] and spirit [soul]. These are not two separate natures, but "their union forms a single nature."[168] The soul leaves the body behind at death. For those who live in Christ, the soul is reunited with a glorified body at the final resurrection.

The soul is the source and seat of human consciousness, identity, intellect, and free will. Each human soul is individual, immortal, and created by God. Prior to birth, the soul is in potential form. At our death, the soul continues to inherit our psychology, so to speak, and "remembers" the choices made in this life and the orientation of the will. The soul is the *persistent self*—in this life and the afterlife, which has implications for the existence and work of purgatory.

Christian anthropology is the branch of theology that explores what it means to be human given the divine plan for our full participation in the beatific vision. How does Christian anthropology fold into philosophical arguments for purgatory? According to Judisch, any philosophical argument for purgatory goes something like this:

1) Perfect holiness is required for entrance into heaven.
2) Rarely does anyone achieve perfect holiness in this life.
3) God zapping us into perfect holiness at the moment of death would radically destroy our sense of identity and freedom.
4) Therefore, an intermediate postmortem process must complete the requisite sanctification for heaven.[169]

Catholics, Orthodox Christians, and Protestants all accept the first two points. Most Protestants reject the third point, asserting that for the saved (or redeemed), the soul is made perfect in the "twinkling of an eye," with no additional suffering or "work" to achieve perfect holiness.[170]

The third point is rooted in the soul's persistent self and maintains that an instantaneous, painless zapping to perfection would violate this requisite human characteristic of the soul. The soul's sense of identity or "personality" must be preserved during and after spiritual transformation, as is required in Catholic teaching.

Human beings are temporal beings. Time acquires a different meaning at death when we step into eternity. The linear, sequential, and quantitative aspects of time stop for us. We enter God's eternal time. The past and present are not separated as they are now. The unfolding of time has a meaning we can't fully grasp. However, that does not mean we have lost the understanding of our "past" or its impact on us. Our past continues to be part of us.

Thiel writes that "[f]or the blessed dead to be themselves ... they must continue to be persons shaped by the history of sin" and acting "in ways that defeat the burden of sin that they both made and suffered. The negotiation of sin is certainly the business of the dead in purgatory."[171]

Irish Catholic theologian Dermot A. Lane seems to agree with Thiel. Lane writes that in "turning back to God after sin, there will remain within the human personality some of the aftereffects of sin: the inner contradiction embedded in the different layers of human personality between being turned once again to God, and self-centered connections and traces of selfishness that remain after conversion. The fundamental decision for God is something that takes time to unfold, permeate, and transform the whole personality."[172]

Some Protestant theologians and philosophers have advanced Christian anthropological arguments for a postmortem intermediate state, such as purgatory. In 1985, Anglican theologian and philosopher David Brown wrote that there must be either an *abrupt* or *gradual* transition in an intermediate state to take the soul from moral imperfection to perfection at death. But an "abrupt transition in essentially *temporal* beings is inconceivable (emphasis added)."[173]

David Brown, like a growing number of Protestants, believes that human nature rules out any instantaneous zapping into perfect holiness at death. He argues that purgatory must exist if heaven does and makes three arguments to advance his case:

- *Argument from Temporality*—Gradual change in character is "indispensable to intelligible human existence."[174] Even in heaven, Brown says change or growth is inevitable. Here, he agrees with C.S. Lewis, who felt that man's temporality is so integral to human nature that strict timelessness "is inconsistent with resurrection of the body."[175]
- *Argument from Identity*—In heaven, to recognize ourselves, we require continuity with our past; "continuity of memories without continuity of character" disrupts continuity of self-identity.[176] Thus, we would not recognize ourselves if everything was righted in our nature instantly.

- *Argument from Self-acceptance*—The perfection required for heaven requires our free response and cooperation with divine will, just as on earth. To preserve our freedom (a requirement for love), the individual must ascent to "each aspect of the transformation of his character."[177]

Moreover, Brown asserts that there is no way progress in moral development after death to perfection can occur without pain as the person discovers all the wrongful earthly choices opposed to God's will, especially in the case of some venial sins that we didn't even realize were wrong. Interestingly, he says *both* satisfaction and sanctification must be elements of purgatory and that the medieval view had it right.[178]

He concludes that "even God cannot eliminate some of the consequences of penalties accruing due to our wrong-doing, namely the need for their gradual, painful self-discovery. Logic forbids their instantaneous removal."[179]

Forensic Justification and Its Dilemma of Sanctification

In Protestant theology, the perfect holiness required for heaven is a side effect of *forensic justification*, whereby the redeemed are accredited with Christ's righteousness through faith alone. In Catholicism's *infused justification*, the source remains Christ, but the redeemed are responsible for cooperating with God's grace to transform their lives. What Catholicism "accomplishes" in purgatory is accomplished in Protestant theology as an instantaneous, (usually) painless act of God at death. Instant forensic sanctification causes theological, philosophical, and anthropological problems for some modern Protestant philosophers.

Protestant philosopher Justin Barnard describes a breakdown in Protestant theology around the zapping theory. He writes of the *dilemma of sanctification* for those who accept forensic or legal justification—that souls, lacking the perfection necessary, are subsumed into heaven at the moment of death because God instantly has purified them—and calls this view *provisionism*. He recognizes that having saving faith is not the same as having a morally sanctified nature.[180]

Like Brown, Barnard believes that provisionism strains credibility because: 1) there would be a discontinuity in personal identity or consciousness for the believer, as he would not recognize himself, and 2) if God can zap the deceased believer into perfection, without an assault to the personal freedom necessary for love, at death, why does he not do it now?[181] Brown and Barnard would not deny profound earthly conversions like that experienced by St. Paul en route to Damascus, but Paul still struggled against sin and failed. (cf. Acts 9:3-6, 9:7-8, and Rom 7:15-19) Rather, Brown and Barnard have difficulty accepting a profound magic-wand-type conversion at death, where sin is no longer possible, while preserving the soul's free will, reforming its intellect, and simultaneously retaining its identity.

Although Barnard argues vehemently against any model of purgatory that includes punishment, he argues that a Sanctification Model of purgatory is entirely consistent with traditional Protestant theology. Further, Barnard avoids the logical conclusion that God is morally culpable for the evil due to man's freedom that God could have prevented had he zapped man earlier.[182] He argues that death is not the end of the process of sanctification that has begun in this life; we essentially pick up where we left off.

Barnard characterizes Catholic purgatory as a purely backward-looking Satisfaction Model (emphasizing temporal punishment) instead of a forward-looking Sanctification Model emphasizing purification, which he endorses. His objection is important since, in my observation, many Catholics have also adopted an informal provisionism, where the dead are instantly in heaven.

According to Barnard, heaven is distinguished from earth by the absence of evil, and that sin is no longer *possible* in heaven.[183] But how exactly would that happen, given that God completely respects our human freedom in this life? Would that not imply God respects it in the next life? Thus, he concludes that we must be involved in our total transformation if we have not attained sanctification before death, ruling out instantaneous sanctification.

Like Barnard, philosopher Jerry Walls believes that Protestants can affirm a Sanctification Model—a stripped-down version of Catholic purgatory that removes the satisfaction or punitive aspects and retains only the sanctification or purification elements. He says that such a model in no way contradicts their theology, and it "makes better sense of how the remains of sin are purged than the typical

Protestant account that it happens instantly and immediately at or after death."[184]

For Walls and others, a postmortem, instantaneous transformation without our free cooperation is problematic: "If God is willing to dispense with our free cooperation in the next life, it is hard to see why He would not do so now, particularly in the view of the high price of freedom in terms of evil and suffering."[185] Walls' objection is particularly hard to deflect when considering the suffering of babies and children who have not reached the age of reason and have committed no actual sins.

Walls believes that if God takes our freedom seriously in this life, he takes our freedom seriously in the next life. The debate over whether purgatory is taught in the Bible is superseded by the "role of human freedom and cooperation" in personal salvation.[186] In other words, can we truly enter into the beatific vision if we have not actively participated in our cleansing rehabilitation?

Anglican philosopher Eleonore Stump uses her amended version of Harry Frankfurt's hierarchical ordered desires to explain why God is unlikely to zap us into heaven's requisite holiness at death without one's explicit participation.[187] Like St. Paul in Romans 7:15, a believer may desire to be perfectly righteous out of love for God, but his basic lower-order desires get in the way of the higher-order desire that God remake his character. Aligning our higher-order desires and actions with God's righteousness takes time.[188] Stump follows Aquinas, who believed that the process of sanctification begins in this life and finishes in the next.[189]

Stump says that a "general submission to God and an effective desire to let God remake one's character ... is psychologically compatible with stubbornly holding on to any number of sins" because the believer fails to recognize his sins "or perceive they're destructive to the point of truly wishing to be delivered to them."[190] Meeting Jesus, Absolute Truth itself, at the individual judgment, reveals the hidden nature of those character defects (disordered attachment to sins) that need correction. These defects keep the soul separate from the object of its love. At that point, purgatory would surely be something that the soul would perceive as a great mercy from God and that the soul would willingly choose.

In his *Letters to Malcolm, Chiefly on Prayer*, Anglican C.S. Lewis (1898-1963) wrote, "Our souls demand Purgatory, don't they?"[191] He recognized that appealing to God's forgiveness alone does not remove our moral imperfections. Purgatory, for Lewis, demonstrated God's love and commitment to our perfect holiness. In *Mere Christianity*, he writes in the voice of God:

> *'Make no mistake,' He says, 'if you let me, I will make you perfect. ... But if you do not push me away, understand that I am going to see this job through. Whatever suffering it may cost you in your earthly life, whatever inconceivable purification it may cost you after death, whatever it costs Me, I will never rest, nor let you rest, until you are literally perfect.'*[192]

Lewis noted that suffering is likely unavoidable on the road to purification, recalling that the most important lessons learned in his life were often painful.[193] Like C.S. Lewis, philosopher Jerry Walls suspects that moral transformation involves pain—but not like the "lurid descriptions" of purgatory depicted in the Middle Ages inflicted from outside the person, but rather the pain inherent to the process of spiritual growth itself and, as Catholics would say, removing the attachments to sin.

Walls sensed a shift in emphasis in Catholic teaching on purgatory during the 20th century towards a purely Sanctification Model. This shift, he felt, offered "good prospects for an ecumenical version of the doctrine that can be affirmed not only by Catholics but many Protestants as well."[194] Although Walls, Barnard, and other religious philosophers have ushered in a new awareness of purgatory in the non-Catholic community in the 21st century, there has never been a wholly dismissive view of some purgatorial rehabilitation.

Some Protestants thought the reformers were too hasty in disposing of purgatory. Alluding to the aftereffects of the Reformation, Reformed Calvinist Peter T. Forsyth (1848-1921) wrote that throwing away purgatory altogether had been "too much" and that "We threw out the baby with the dirty water of its bath."[195]

In his book *Purgatory: The Logic of Total Transformation*, Walls notes several contemporary Protestant thinkers or theologians sympathetic towards a Sanctification Model of purgatory. Among them are Jurgen Moltmann (b. 1926), who believed that God would continue his merciful work after our death to achieve our purity of heart, especially for those whose lives were cut short; Cambridge physicist turned religious philosopher John Polkinghorne (1930-2021); and Clark Pinnock (1937-2010), who believed that human participation, not some autonomous process, is required for postmortem sanctification.[196]

Protestant theologian John Hicks proposed a postmortem intermediary state where the soul continues on its path of personal growth in preparation for heaven as part of his *soul-making* theory.[197] *Soul-making* is "the belief that the human person was created by God with the intention of achieving perfection through a process of moral and spiritual growth within creation, and that creation itself was designed for the purpose of abetting this growth."[198] Hicks felt that the instantaneous transformation of the individual at death to perfect holiness minimized the significance of this life and left no justification for evil in the world for a good God.

In this chapter, we have speculated on the "work" of purgatory within the guidelines of the Church's dogma and further constrained by what it means to be a human being with continuity of self in the afterlife. We have borrowed insights from Catholic theologians, Protestant theologians, and Protestant philosophers. Next, we turn our attention to the fascinating history of purgatory.

7 – THE HISTORY OF PURGATORY

For centuries, purgatory did not need an official stamp, because it had gradually seeped into common Christian understanding of where the dead Christians went.[199]
Isabel Moreira

The history of purgatory is complex and contentious. Protestants and Catholics have seemingly opposite theological stakes in the doctrine, while secular historians interpret purgatory's history from a socio-economic viewpoint.[200]

Jacques Le Goff, a respected secular historian, argued that profound social and economic changes coupled with the increased population of the high Middle Ages created the perfect climate for purgatory to take root and tags its formal "birth certificate" to around the 12th century.[201] He rejects the idea that purgatory evolved from the practice of penance, prayers for the dead, and the Church's greater understanding of sin and its temporal consequences.

The earliest Christians expected Jesus to return in their lifetimes; thus, an intermediate state, such as purgatory, received little thought. However, with the delay of Christ's second coming, the early Church's focus broadened. For the individual Christian, the focus intensified on the limited years one had to live, avoiding sin, and growing in virtue. "With this more compact and personalized eschatology, the believer's death now became the focal point of judgment, a death packed with all the moments of life that fell under the divine scrutiny for which the believer was held accountable."[202]

Biblical Exegesis and Apocryphal Literature

Pope Benedict XVI, writing as Joseph Ratzinger, asserted that "the New Testament left open the question of the 'intermediate state' between death and the general resurrection of the Last Day" and "remained in an unfinished condition, since it could only be clarified by the gradual unfolding of Christian anthropology and its relation to Christology."[203] With time, that intermediate state would come to be called purgatory.

For many devout and sincere Protestants, purgatory remains a false Catholic construct, especially since the Bible does not explicitly contain the word *purgatory*. While no New Testament Scripture explicitly mentions purgatory, several verses have been consistently exegeted over the centuries to motivate its theological development. Entire books have been dedicated to scriptural "proofs" of purgatory.[204]

Such "proofs" hardly convince someone not already positively predisposed to believe in purgatory, as reading and interpreting Scripture is influenced by the individual's denominational perspective. As philosopher Brian Cross observed, what passes for objective analysis often assumes the truth or falsehood of the argument one proposes to evaluate.[205] This understandable bias does not mean we should ignore Scripture, but rather that we should be aware of the human tendency to go fishing for Scripture to support our already preconceived notions (especially when they oppose Church teaching). This "muffling" of the gentle voice of the Holy Spirit is an inherent danger in *sola Scriptura*.

Since the Protestant Reformation, Christians have used many Scriptures to *disprove* the existence of purgatory.[206] The common thread running through these "disproof" texts is that the Christian is already made justified, blameless, and cleansed by faith alone in Christ's redeeming work. The sins that God has forgiven, he has forgotten and hence won't "punish" the redeemed for them in purgatory.

The most common "disproof" text is Luke 23:43, where Jesus tells the Good Thief at his crucifixion, "Today you will be with me in Paradise." The argument goes something like this: 1) The Good Thief was guilty of some sin by his admission (*We indeed have been condemned justly, for we are getting what we deserve for our deeds*); 2) the Good Thief professed his faith in Christ as King (*Jesus, remember me when you come into your kingdom*); 3) Jesus said the Good Thief would go to heaven "today" (*Today you will be with me in Paradise*); 4) therefore, there can be no purgatory because the Good Thief went straight to heaven. This disproof analysis assumes forensic justification by faith alone but primarily hinges on the word *today*.

Whatever time is like after death, it is not time as we know it, nor can we conceive of it except in the abstract. As death opens the door to eternity for us, could not time be simply one eternal today? In death, we step outside of time and exist wholly in the present of God's time.[207] God's time is eternity; it is "the center of all things" from which "all things proceed, [and] to it all things return."[208]

But setting aside the mystery of time in the afterlife, we can imagine that in the Good Thief's encounter with Christ, he had perfect contrition for his past sins, made atonement by accepting his punishment, and received a Baptism of desire in the Spirit in his "yes" to Jesus. As Catholics, we believe Baptism wipes out all vestiges of sin, original and actual. Lastly, we must remember that God is bound only by his nature of pure love. Although we "know" God through Scripture and the image of him through the Son, God is mysteriously incomprehensible. We do not limit the extravagance of God's ways by our small-minded understanding.

The early Latin and Greek Church Fathers used numerous biblical passages to argue for a postmortem state (or place) of purgation. However, the four most commonly cited are 1 Corinthians 3:11-15, Matthew 5:25-26, Matthew 12:32, and 2 Maccabees 12:42-45. We will examine each in turn.

By far, the most utilized Scripture is 1 Corinthians 3:11-15.[209] Here, St. Paul encourages the Corinthians to build their lives upon the teachings of Christ so that on the day of judgment, even if some of their works failed divine scrutiny (burned up), they would be saved (but only as through fire).

> *For no one can lay any foundation other than the one that has been laid; that foundation is Jesus Christ. Now if anyone builds on the foundation with gold, silver, precious stones, wood, hay, straw—the work of each builder will become visible, for the Day will disclose it, because it will be revealed with fire, and the fire will test what sort of work each has done. If what has been built on the foundation survives, the builder will receive a reward. If the work is burned up, the builder will suffer loss; the builder will be saved, but only as through fire.*

That "the builder will be saved, but only as through fire" seemed to indicate that the faithful Christian, dying with imperfect works (or sin), might have to endure some rather unpleasant purging or expiation in the afterlife. 1 Corinthians 3:11-15 was also used to distinguish lesser or venial sin (where the builder was saved) from grievous or mortal sin (where the builder was not saved). The *Catechism of the Catholic Church* references these verses and 1 Peter 1:6-7 (*tested by fire*) in the pages dedicated to "The Final Purification, or Purgatory."[210]

Another commonly exegeted Scripture was Matthew 5:25-26.[211] In this parable, Jesus warns the accused to come quickly to terms with his accuser before meeting the judge. This was interpreted as meeting Christ at the individual judgment.

> *Come to terms quickly with your accuser while you are on the way to court with him, or your accuser may hand you over to the judge, and the judge to the guard, and you will be thrown into prison. Truly I tell you, you will never get out until you have paid the last penny[.]*

The words: *judge, court, prison*, and *paid the last penny* motivated the Christian to complete the penance for his sins while on earth and not after death. The prison represented purgatory, while the last penny was the temporal punishment for lesser sins and repented but forgiven grave sins.

Another text, Matthew 12:32, was used to argue for purgation in the world to come.[212] Here, Jesus says:

> *Whoever speaks a word against the Son of Man will be forgiven, but whoever speaks against the Holy Spirit will not be forgiven, either in this age or in the age to come.*

It was reasoned that if some sins *could not be* forgiven in the age to come, then there must be some sins that *could be* forgiven in the age to come—in purgatory. The Church tied penance to the forgiveness of sins, so there must be an opportunity to do penance between death and the last judgment. Although the *Catechism of the Catholic Church* does not cite Matthew 12:32 in its exposition of purgatory, it was important in the writings of the early Church Fathers.

That the living can intercede for the dead is linked to purgatory in the *Catechism of the Catholic Church* in §1032. Logically, this association makes sense. The belief in an intermediate state *does not* necessitate acceptance that the living can pray for the dead. But the belief that the living can pray for the dead *does* require belief in the existence in some intermediate state, for those in hell are beyond help, and those in heaven need no help.

An Old Testament text, 2 Maccabees 12:42-45, provides a window into the practice of praying for the dead in the Jewish community. Around 150-120 BC, Judas Maccabee took up a "sin offering" collection to atone for the fallen Jewish soldiers who had died wearing a token of an idol under their clothing, a serious offense against the first commandment given to Moses:

> *He also took up a collection, man by man, to the amount of two thousand drachmas of silver, and sent it to Jerusalem to provide for a sin offering. In doing this he acted very well and honorably, taking account of the resurrection. For if he were not expecting that those who had fallen would rise again, it would have been superfluous and foolish to pray for the dead.*

While Martin Luther removed the Second Book of Maccabees and six others from the Protestant Bible, the verses above provide historical evidence that some Jews prayed for the dead and offered sacrifices to God to atone for the sins of the deceased. Because prayers for the dead make no sense if the soul is in heaven or hell, Christians have from earliest times connected these verses to the efficacy of suffrages for the souls in an intermediate place (or state) like purgatory. Even today, Orthodox Jewish men pray the Kaddish for eleven Hebrew months after the death of their fathers.

Evidence that the early Christian communities prayed for their beloved dead is apparent from surviving grave marker inscriptions in the catacombs. The inscriptions request that the deceased be given refreshment (*refrigerium*),[213] analogous to the familiar refrain, may their soul rest in peace.

Before 313 AD, during the time of persecution, pagan and Christian grave marker inscriptions may be compared. While both contain marked affections for the deceased, unique to the Christian inscriptions was a "firm belief in the reality of a future life: they pray for the dead as though they were still living, and capable of feeling joy and sorrow; or they call upon them for assistance as though they were still able to give it;[214] and often the very language in which they speak of death and all that concerns it bears within it an unconscious testimony to faith in a future resurrection."[215]

Apocryphal writings also bear testimony to the early Christian practice of prayers for the dead. The *Acts of St. Paul and Thecla*, literature from the late 2nd century, indicate a belief in the efficacy of prayers for the dead:

> *[A]nd behold, the daughter of Trifina, who was dead, appeared to her mother* [in a dream], *and said, "Mother, let the young woman, Thecla, be reputed by you as your daughter in my stead; and desire her that she should pray for me, that I may be translated to a state of happiness."*[216]

Another commonly cited example of prayers for the dead in early Christian literature comes from The *Martyrdom of Perpetua and Felicity* (c.203), attributed to Tertullian or someone in his circle. Perpetua, while awaiting her martyrdom, prays for her deceased brother Dinocrates. In this work, the author recounts Perpetua's inspiration to pray for her brother, seemingly confirmed in a dream shortly after, whereby she realizes that her brother is suffering. Then, after she makes "supplication for him day and night with groans and tears," she is assured of his relief by a final dream: "I awoke. Then I understood that he was translated from his pains."[217]

There is a strong connection between "what is prayed" and "what is believed." Grave inscriptions and apocryphal literature support an early Christian belief in the efficacy of prayers for the dead and a strong connection between the living and the dead. These beliefs are logically consistent with a postmortem intermediate "place" that isn't heaven or hell.

Traditions and Maturation of Theological Thought

The writing of the Church Fathers moved purgatory's theology forward from grave marker inscriptions and apocryphal literature to its eventual proclamation as Catholic dogma in the late Middle Ages. Important influencers were Clement of Alexandria (c.150-c.215), Cyprian of Carthage (c.200-258), Augustine of Hippo (354-430), Gregory the Great (540-604), Bede the Venerable (c.673-735), Boniface (c.675-754), and the contributions of the Scholastics—theologically and logic-driven philosophers—during the high Middle Ages, including Thomas Aquinas (1225-1274).

The Greek and Latin Fathers (2nd-7th Century)

Clement of Alexandria was a theologian, philosopher, and convert to Christianity.[218] According to Pope Benedict XVI, writing as Joseph Ratzinger, Clement saw penance as a process "which can and often must continue beyond the gate of death."[219] In his *Stromata*, Clement wrote of postmortem "expiation and purification" for sins committed after Baptism. This discipline was temporary, not eternal, before "the pure vision of insatiable contemplation."[220] Moreover, Clement believed that one's membership in the Church continued with its interpersonal connection into the afterlife, where burdens could still be shared between the living and the dead.

During the Roman persecution, Cyprian of Carthage (c. 210-258) faced the challenge of reinstating Christians who had denied their faith when faced with torture or martyrdom. Cyprian devised a plan of rigorous penitential purification whereby the "half-hearted" Christians could be brought back into communion with the Church. Based on his interpretation of Matthew 5:25-26, Cyprian decided that if a penitent died before completing his penance, he could finish it in the afterlife. According to philosopher Jerry Walls, Cyprian's view on postmortem penance was a significant step in the development of purgatory.[221]

In 313 AD, the Roman persecution of Christians stopped under Emperor Constantine. "Red" martyrdom, marked by the spilling of blood, was replaced by "white" martyrdom with the rise of asceticism, self-denial, and penitential acts to scale the heights of Christian discipleship. "Christians sought an alternative understanding of saintly imitation and found it in the nascent ascetical movement," providing a fertile environment for contemplating the value of penance in this life and the life to come.[222]

During this time, Augustine of Hippo (354-430) laid the critical foundation for the theological development of purgatory in the Latin Church. Historian Jacques Le Goff calls Augustine the "true father of purgatory."[223] Augustine introduced the terminology that would influence the tone and inspire the writing through the Middle Ages: *poenae purgatoriae* (purgatorial punishments) and *poenae temporariae* (temporary punishments) for those who were not bad enough for hell but not good enough for heaven.

Augustine was the first to make an explicit connection between punishment and purgation, which would influence the formal doctrine of purgatory a thousand years later.[224] In his book, *City of God*, Augustine asserted that divine punishments were purifying to those who accepted the punishments as corrective discipline and amended their lives, but not for others who refused the corrective discipline. Augustine wrote that God's punishments were due to past or present sins and sometimes to mature the person in grace:

> *[E]ven in this life some punishments are purgatorial—not, indeed, to those whose life is none the better, but rather the worse for them, but to those who are constrained by them to amend their life. All other punishments, whether temporal or eternal, inflicted as they are on everyone by divine providence, are sent either on account of past sins, or of sins presently allowed in the life, or to exercise and reveal a man's graces.*[225]

In the same work, Augustine distinguished between 1) temporary punishments in this life and after death and 2) temporary postmortem punishments and eternal punishment:

> *But temporary punishments are suffered by some in this life only, by others after death, by others both now and then; but all of them before that last and strictest judgment. But of those who suffer temporary punishments after death, all are not doomed to those everlasting pains which are to follow that judgment; for to some, as we have already said, what is not remitted in this world is remitted in the next, that is, they are not punished with the eternal punishment of the world to come.*[226]

Le Goff credits Augustine with the "infernalization of purgatory," a theme much echoed centuries later in medieval art and writing.[227] Augustine wrote in his *Commentary on Psalm 38* (in conjunction with 1 Corinthians 3:11-15) that "though we should be 'saved by fire,' yet will that fire be more grievous than anything that man can suffer in this life whatsoever."[228]

St. Gregory the Great (540-604) wrote the four books of his *Dialogues* several months after he was made pope. Widely read in the Middle Ages, "the first rudiments of the medieval conception of the three states of souls in the other world" are found and would impact the development of purgatory.[229] In his fourth book, Gregory uses 1 Corinthians 3:11-15 (as did Augustine) in conjunction with Matthew 12:32 to argue for purgation in the world to come.

In the lengthy excerpt below, Gregory describes purgatory as distinct from tribulations in this life. He attributes only minor sins to the souls in purgatory, which we recognize in the Church's teaching as venial sins. In contrast, Gregory writes that the guilt of "greater sorts of sins" can't be forgiven in purgatory.

> *[M]an departeth out of this life, in the same he is presented in judgment before God. But yet we must believe that before the day of judgment there is a Purgatory fire for certain small sins: because our Saviour saith, that*

he which speaketh blasphemy against the holy Ghost, that it shall not be forgiven him, neither in this world, nor in the world to come. Out of which sentence we learn, that some sins are forgiven in this world, and some other may be pardoned in the next: for that which is denied concerning one sin, is consequently understood to be granted touching some other. But yet this, as I said, we have not to believe but only concerning little and very small sins, ... ignorant errors in matters of no great weight: all which sins be punished after death, if men procured not pardon and remission for them in their lifetime: for when St. Paul saith, that Christ is the foundation: and by and by addeth: And if any man build upon this foundation gold, silver, precious stones, wood, hay, stubble: the work of everyone, of what kind it is, the fire shall try. If any man's work abide which he built thereupon, he shall receive reward; if any man's work burn, he shall suffer detriment, but himself shall be saved, yet so as by fire. For although these words may be understood of the fire of tribulation, which men suffer in this world: yet if any will interpret them of the fire of Purgatory, which shall be in the next life: then must he carefully consider, that the Apostle said not that he may be saved by fire, that buildeth upon this foundation iron, brass, or lead, that is, the greater sort of sins, and therefore more hard, and consequently not remissible in that place: but wood, hay, stubble, that is, little and very light sins, which the fire doth easily consume. Yet we have here further to consider, that none can be there purged, no, not for the least sins that be, unless in his lifetime he deserved by virtuous works to find such favour in that place.[230]

In the story of the monk Justus, found in Gregory's Dialogues, the tradition of Gregorian Masses—thirty Masses on consecutive days to help liberate the soul of the deceased—finds its genesis.[231]

Missionary Monks (6th-7th Century)

Historian Isabel Moreira believes that by the time of Venerable Bede (c.672–735) and St. Boniface (c.675-754), the idea of purgatory was well established and that prayers for the dead were believed to cut short the soul's experience of purgatorial fires. She bases this on surviving literary evidence of a letter written by Boniface and several extant sermons by Bede.[232] Both were English Benedictine monks and contemporaries, although it is unknown if they ever met.

Boniface is known for his missionary efforts in Germany and eventual martyrdom by pagans in the Netherlands. Bede was a highly respected and skilled translator, editor, historian, sermon writer, and theologian.

Boniface wrote of a monk, while Bede wrote of a layman named Drythelm, who had visions of visiting a purgatory-like "place" inhabited by the dead during what we might term today as near-death experiences. In the *Vision of the Monk of Wenlock* by Boniface and the *Vision of Drythelm* by Bede, historian Moreira writes that "[n]either writer commented that he was introducing something new or speculative, and it is unlikely that either thought he was breaking new ground."[233]

Boniface interviewed the monk and documented his vision in a letter to a nun. When close to heaven, the monk saw souls moving across a bridge spanning a river of boiling pitch to Jerusalem. Those who fell into the river were purified from the filth of minor sins and emerged more beautiful and brilliant than previously.[234]

In Bede's work, after the layman Drythelm had died and been resuscitated by his wife, he reported seeing souls unable to enter heaven because they were insufficiently purified despite their good works. Valleys of fire and ice tormented the souls due to "inadequate and delayed penance," yet they were assured of heaven. Drythelm's angel guide assured him this was not hell as he had thought initially. Additionally, Drythelm learned that the prayers of the faithful could assist the souls in their journey to heaven.[235] Bede believed that visions had their place in religious instruction if properly edited. His impressive credentials lent authority to the *Vision of Drythelm*, which had circulated before Bede put pen to paper.

According to Moreira, it was the homilies of Bede that moved purgatory into mainstream church teaching as a response to the heresy of Origen (c.185–c.253) regarding universal salvation.[236] Bede preached that salvation was possible for those with serious sins after a sincere and worthy reception of the Sacrament of Confession and the completion of their assigned penance. Purgation in the afterlife began to offer hope for the Christian by satisfying God's judgment, especially when he fell again into sin.

In a critical piece of scholarship, Moreira presents a sermon Bede prepared for Advent, dated between 720 and 730. Here, Bede writes that those still "polluted" by their evil works "went out from their body after death to be severely chastised, and seized by the flames of the fire of Purgatory *[flammis ignis purgatorii]*." There, they are "made clean of the stain of their vices" and remain until Judgement

Day unless relieved of their penalties by the "petitions, almsgiving, fasting, weeping, and oblation of the saving sacrificial offering of their faithful friends."[237]

As Moreira asserts, all the elements were in place, although perhaps crude, for purgatory's eventual elevation to dogma in the Roman Catholic Church. She writes that in "Bede's *Vision of Drythelm*, we find a fully developed description of purgatory as a location in the otherworld that is temporary, punitive, but available to the intercession of the church and the intervention of the living."[238]

Some four centuries later, this prayerful connection between the living and the dead was further integrated into Church practice when the monks at the Abbey of Cluny in France first observed All Souls' Day (originally called the Day of the Dead) between 1024 and 1033.

The Scholastic Influence (12th-13th Century)

Scholasticism was the predominant method of thought and instruction in universities between 1100-1500. Characterized by dialectical reasoning, the Scholastics married the logic of Greek philosophy to theology. This style of teaching and writing is evident in Aquinas's *Summa Theologica*. Karen Palmer summarizes the assumptions of Scholastic Theology as,

- *God is real.*
- *It is possible to know God.*
- *God wants people to know Him.*
- *He has given people Revelation so that they might know Him.*
- *He has left clues throughout creation about Himself.*
- *Science and Theology are both ways of comprehending God.*
- *Theology interprets Revelation and tells people what to believe.*
- *Science interprets Creation to show how God does things.* [239]

Through the discourse and writings of the Scholastics, purgatory received firm theological standing. The living remain connected to the souls in purgatory and are encouraged to intercede for the souls and help mitigate their suffering.

By the 12th century, purgation in the afterlife was accepted as part of the Church's teaching with no substantial addition to the basic attributes formulated by Augustine and Gregory the Great:

temporary, painful, a "hidden receptacle" for souls with lesser sins or already-forgiven grave sin for those not bad enough for hell but not ready for heaven, and with suffrages of the living able to help the dead. But purgatory did not yet have the stamp of dogmatic declaration.

In *The Birth of Purgatory*, secular historian Jacques Le Goff argues that the profound social and economic changes, coupled with the spike in population of the high Middle Ages, created favorable conditions for the formal "birth" of purgatory. Between 1170 and 1180, he concludes that purgatory was first used as a noun by Peter Comestor (a student of Peter Lombard) in the school of Notre Dame in Paris.[240]

Before Comestor, Le Goff asserts that the word occurred only as an adjective (e.g., purgatorial fire) in the original Latin texts. According to Le Goff, one finds the Latin form of the noun only after the late 12th century. In the original texts, he wrote that the usage occurs as an adjective, such as *poenae purgatoriae* (purgatorial punishments), but not as the noun *purgatorium, purgatorio, or purgatorii* (purgatory). [241]

This difference, adjective versus noun, is critical to Le Goff's claim that the theology of purgatory was a novel product of the Scholastic theological movement of the late Middle Ages. We have seen, however, that Moreira's recent (and less known) evidence has refuted Le Goff's claim through Bede's use of *flammis ignis purgatorii*. What remains correct is that purgatory's theology became stabilized and precise through the work of the Scholastics—an artifact of that being its predictable usage as a noun.

Gratian of Bologna (d.1144-1145), a Benedictine monk, emphasized the role that the living have in easing and shortening the sufferings of the souls undergoing purgation. In his *Decretum*, a corpus of medieval canon law, Gratian wrote that the "souls of the deceased are redeemed in four ways, either by the offerings of the priests, or by the prayers of the saints, or by alms-giving, or by the fasting of relatives."[242] This teaching found in the *Decretum* remained unchanged from the time of St. Augustine and St. Gregory the Great.

The 13th-century Scholastics, Franciscans Alexander of Hales (c.1185-1245) and St. Bonaventure (1221-1274) along with Dominicans St. Albert the Great (c1200-1280) and St. Thomas Aquinas (1225–1274) systematized purgatory. They incorporated the work of St. Augustine and specified all the features of purgatory that would eventually become dogma.[243]

Le Goff emphasized the role of Alexander Hales in connecting the suffrages of the living to aid in the expiation and satisfaction for the sins of the suffering souls in purgatory. These suffrages, Hales wrote, added to the "merits" of the Church.[244] The role of the living in contributing to the *Treasury of Merits* will be incorporated into the *Communion of the Saints*, critical for the theology of indulgences of Chapter 9.

As to the nature of the suffering in purgatory, Bonaventure distinguished between the material fire of satisfaction (punitive) and a spiritual fire of purgation (cleansing).[245] Like the other Scholastics, he emphasized the power of prayer and suffrages for the dead because they can no longer acquire merit for themselves.

Albert the Great saw purgatory as a place of hope and focused more on "purgation than on the penalties."[246] He did not believe that a soul necessarily must stay in purgatory for a long time, especially if aided by the suffrages of the living. He is credited with controlling the popular imagination as he threw the torturing demons out of purgatory and placed its location closer to heaven than hell.

Thomas Aquinas was the most influential of the Scholastics. He believed, as had Augustine, that the pain of purgatory would exceed that of anything on earth. This understanding facilitated the laity's positive reception of indulgences to spare their loved ones such pain.

Aquinas's articulate philosophy and theology tremendously affected Catholic dogma, doctrine, and teaching in many areas, including purgatory. The dual nature of sin on the soul (turning the sinner's heart away from God and the debt of temporal punishment) cemented the dual character of purgatory as both penalty (Satisfaction Model) and purgation (Sanctification Model):

> *Two things are required for the perfect cleansing from sins, corresponding to the two things comprised in sin—namely, the stain of sin and the debt of punishment. The stain of sin is, indeed, blotted out by grace, by which the sinner's heart is turned to God: whereas the debt of punishment is entirely removed by the satisfaction that man offers to God.*[247]

Although Aquinas died before finishing his *Summa Theologica*, his students transcribed his teachings on purgatory, found in the *Summa's* appendices.

> *[I]t is sufficiently clear that there is a Purgatory after this life. For if the debt of punishment is not paid in full after the stain of sin has been*

washed away by contrition, nor again are venial sins always removed when mortal sins are remitted, and if justice demands that sin be set in order by due punishment, it follows that one who after contrition for his fault and after being absolved, dies before making due satisfaction, is punished after this life.[248]

Papal and Magisterial Documents

The earliest church documents to use the noun *purgatory* are found in papal letters. Although these letters do *not* constitute dogma, they open a window into the prevalent teaching on the intermediate state in the Latin Church and expose the tensions between Latin and Greek Christians regarding purgatory.

Three ecumenical councils addressed purgatory between the thirteenth and the sixteenth centuries. In the last two councils, purgatory takes its complete dogmatic form, virtually unchanged in tone in formal church documents until the *Catechism of the Catholic Church*, published at the turn of the 21st century.

Pre-Dogma Documents (13th-15th Century)

While the Latin Roman Catholic Church refined its teaching on purgatory, the Greek Orthodox Church had some issues. The Greeks endorsed the efficacy of prayers of the dead and postmortem purification. However, postmortem purification held no hint of punishment for the Greeks and did not take place in an intermediate place separate from heaven as for the Latins. Disagreement between the Latin and Greek Church was not new; the two arms first split in the Great Schism of 1054.[249] The Roman Catholic understanding of purgatory was one of several theological issues disrupting the unity with the Greeks.

Although the word *purgatory* was already in mainstream usage by the Scholastics, the first occurrence in a papal document occurred in a personal letter by Pope Innocent IV to the Greek Church in Cypress (Tusculum) sent in 1254. The Pope hoped to nudge the Greeks to a common belief in purgatory with the Latin Church and that they accept the usage of the term *purgatory*. After exegeting 1 Corinthians 3:13-15 and Matthew 12:32 and emphasizing the beliefs held in common, Innocent IV wrote:

> [W]e indeed, calling it purgatory according to the traditions and authority of the Holy Fathers, wish that in the future it be called by that name in their area. For in that transitory fire certainly sins, though not criminal or capital, which before have not been remitted through penance but were small and minor sins, are cleansed, and these weigh heavily even after death, if they have been forgiven in this life.[250]

Innocent IV borrowed St. Augustine's "transitory fire" and linked the cleansing of purgatory to sins for which sufficient penance had been accomplished before death. Elements of purification and expiation are both present.

During the Second Council of Lyons [1272-1274], bishops from the Latin and the Greek Church convened together under Pope Gregory X. The primary topics were reclaiming the Holy Land from the Muslim conquest and reunifying the Church. To the latter goal, the council decreed in 1274 that the souls of repentant sinners who die in charity without fully executing penance for their sins are purified after death. Perhaps in a conciliatory measure, the word *purgatory* was avoided.[251]

> [If] those who after baptism slip into sin ... die truly repentant in charity before they have made satisfaction by worthy fruits of penance for (sins) committed and omitted, their souls are cleansed after death by purgatorial or purifying punishments ... [a]nd to relieve punishments of this kind, the offerings of the living faithful are of advantage to these, namely, the sacrifices of Masses, prayers, alms, and other duties of piety[.][252]

The wording embraced both satisfaction (expiation) and purifying functions, with the punishments effecting the purification. The Council did not refer to any "fire," and suffrages for the dead were endorsed. Although the Council members ratified the language, the unification was brief; the Orthodox clergy rejected the resolution shortly afterward.

In 1351, Pope Clement VI (1342-1352) sent a letter to the bishop of the Armenians, who were part of the Greek Church. In calling the Armenians to the traditions and beliefs of the Latin Church, Clement VI rekindled the "fire" of purgatory to achieve the satisfaction and cleansing functions as had Pope Innocent IV in the century previous:

> [T]here is a purgatory to which depart the souls of those dying in grace who have not yet made complete satisfaction for their sins ... they will be tortured by fire for a time and that as soon as they are cleansed, even

before the day of judgment, they may come to the true and eternal beatitude which consists in the vision of God face to face and in love.[253]

Neither the 1351 letter of Clement VI nor the 1254 letter of Innocent IV were drafted and ratified as part of an ecumenical council. Notably, the Second Council of Lyons's declaration on purgatory, convened between the two letters, avoided the "infernalization" language as would all other ecumenical councils to come.

During the Council of Florence in 1439, Pope Eugenius IV affirmed in *Laetentur Caeli* (Heaven Rejoices) everything from the Second Council of Lyons: the cleansing and expiatory punishments of purgatory and the intercessory power of the faithful.

> *[I]f those truly penitent have departed in the love of God, before they have made satisfaction by worthy fruits of penance for sins of commission and omission, the souls of these are cleansed after death by purgatorial punishments; and so that they may be released from punishments of this kind, the suffrages of the living faithful are of advantage to them, namely, the sacrifices of Masses, prayers, and almsgiving, and other works of piety, which are customarily performed by the faithful for other faithful according to the institutions of the Church.*[254]

The Church would unambiguously elevate this teaching to dogma at the Council of Trent in response to the various heresies sparked by the Protestant Reformation, triggered in 1517 by Martin Luther.[255] Trent would assert no new teachings on purgatory but would declare the doctrine as a matter of faith by the power of apostolic authority.

Dogmatic Declarations (16th Century)

The Council of Trent was held in three parts, convening under several different popes and extending over eighteen years beginning in 1545. From a doctrinal viewpoint, the Council of Trent was one of the most important councils in the Roman Catholic Church, "fixing her distinctive faith and practice in relation to the Protestant Evangelical churches."[256] Trent would shape the path of orthodox teaching until Vatican II.[257]

The growing popularity of the Protestant view of *forensic* justification versus the Catholic view of *infused* justification (requiring human cooperation with grace) had eroded the Church's teachings on purgatory. During Session Six of Trent, the Council issued thirty-three summary teachings (or *canons*) on justification.

A deviation in tone is apparent between The Council of Trent's documents and those from previous council documents. Trent's tenor is firm, negative, and nonconciliatory as dogma and the teaching authority of the Latin Church were at stake. The Council of Trent began the much-needed Catholic Counter-Reformation (1548-c.1700). But by then, the animosity between Catholics and Protestants was intense and continued to gather strength. The documents "were often expressed in ways that made the Catholic Church's teachings as distinct from Protestant positions as possible."[258]

Trent's many documents reinforced and reiterated Catholic teachings disputed by the Protestant reformers, including how the faithful are justified and sanctified. The Council also condemned the sale and abuse of indulgences. Two documents from Trent are essential to the discussion of purgatory: *Decree on Justification: Canon 30*, issued on Jan 13, 1547, and the *Decree Concerning Purgatory* from Session 25 on December 4, 1563.

Three centuries before Trent, the Scholastic theologians, especially Aquinas, had formalized the concept of temporal punishment in Catholic teaching. Trent's Canon 30 reinforced the idea of temporal punishment due to sins—critical to the theology of purgatory:

If anyone says that after the reception of the grace of justification the guilt is so remitted and the debt of eternal punishment so blotted out to every repentant sinner, that no debt of temporal punishment remains to be discharged either in this world or in purgatory before the gates of heaven can be opened, let him be anathema. [259]

In the last session of the third part of the Council of Trent convened under Pope Pius IV, the Council reaffirmed the declarations from the Council of Florence on purgatory pronounced more than a century before.

Whereas the Catholic Church, instructed by the Holy Ghost, has, from the sacred writings and the ancient tradition of the Fathers, taught, in sacred councils, and very recently in this ecumenical Synod, that there is a Purgatory, and that the souls there detained are helped by the suffrages of the faithful, but principally by the acceptable sacrifice of the altar; the holy Synod enjoins on bishops that they diligently endeavor that the sound doctrine concerning Purgatory, transmitted by the holy Fathers and sacred councils, be believed, maintained, taught, and everywhere proclaimed by the faithful of Christ. But let the more difficult and subtle questions, and which tend not to edification, and from which for the most part there is no increase of piety, be excluded from popular discourses before the uneducated multitude. In like manner, such things as are uncertain, or which labor under an appearance of error, let them not allow to be made public and treated of. While those things which tend to a certain kind of curiosity or superstition, or which savor of filthy lucre, let them prohibit as scandals and stumbling blocks of the faithful. But let the bishops take care, that the suffrages of the faithful who are living, to wit the sacrifices of masses, prayers, alms, and other works of piety, which have been wont to be performed by the faithful for the other faithful departed, be piously and devoutly performed, in accordance with the institutes of the church; and that whatsoever is due on their behalf, from the endowments of testators, or in other way, be discharged, not in a perfunctory manner, but diligently and accurately, by the priests and ministers of the church, and others who are bound to render this (service).[260]

Trent's *Decree Concerning Purgatory* declared and affirmed:
1. Purgatory as an infallible dogma.
2. Purgatory's connection to the teaching and traditions of the Church Fathers and the Council of Lyons II and Florence.
3. The efficacy of the suffrages, especially the Mass, for the souls in purgatory.
4. That the clergy piously and devoutly perform intercessions for the souls in purgatory.
5. The bishops' responsibility is to teach the (largely uneducated) faithful about purgatory, avoiding "curiosities or superstitions" that might confuse them.
6. No tolerance for any sale of indulgences.

The Church's teachings on purgatory remain the same to this day. However, one encounters a much-softened tone in the three paragraphs in the *Catechism of the Catholic Church* on purgatory (§1030-§1032). And notably, "punishment" is only used as a contrast point to hell [§1031]. That purgatory exists as dogma is an example of a *fides ecclesiastica* dogma and is due, in no small part, to the theological storm unleashed by Martin Luther's *95 Theses* (1517).

Next, we look at what indulgences are in Chapter 8. Their history and their impact on the Protestant Reformation is treated separately in Chapter 9.

8 – INDULGENCES & THEIR CONNECTION TO PURGATORY

Reconciliation with God does not mean that there are no enduring consequences of sin from which we must be purified. It is precisely in this context that the indulgence becomes important, since it is an expression of the total gift of the mercy of God. With the indulgence, the repentant sinner receives a remission of the temporal punishment due for the sins already forgiven[.][261]

Pope St. John Paul II

Informally, we can think of indulgences as an extension of prayers and pious intercessory actions to assist souls in purgatory, provided certain conditions are met. These diverse actions, or *works of satisfaction*, could include, among others, praying the Rosary, Eucharistic adoration, reading Scripture, or making the Stations of the Cross. The Church provides concrete examples of indulged acts and prayers in the *Manual of Indulgences*.[262]

Philosophically, one may affirm the existence of purgatory while rejecting and denying indulgences. Theologically, however, the Church's dogma on indulgences automatically presumes the dogma of purgatory and the doctrine of temporal punishment due to sin.

In the *Catechism of the Catholic Church,* purgatory remains tightly linked to indulgences, though indulgences are *not* a required Catholic practice.[263] Their histories are intertwined. Thus, examining the doctrine and history of indulgences is not a detour but part of our journey to rediscover purgatory.

The model of purgatory in the Catholic Church contains elements of expiation and purification; we may ask how indulgences might serve each function in charity. For example, might indulgences substitute for some part of the deceased's remaining temporal punishments, or might they expedite the spiritual and moral growth process for the soul undergoing purgation? The Church does not speculate, just as it does not say precisely how God readies the soul for heaven in purgatory.

Although purgatory is logically distinct from indulgences, the two remain lumped together in the minds of many Protestant Christians.[264] History attributes the catalyst for Martin Luther's *95 Theses* and the ensuing Protestant Reformation to the "sale of indulgences." Thus, we would be remiss to ignore indulgences and their history.

Whether the Catholic Church sold indulgences or not fails to *invalidate* purgatory or indulgences in the same way that abuses of political freedom do not invalidate democracy or a priest in a state of mortal sin does not invalidate the sacraments he confers.[265] Rather, the abuses associated with indulgences *validate* the pervasive human tendency to sin. St. Augustine is reputed to have remarked that the Church is a raw diamond held in dirty hands.[266]

Many Christians object to indulgences for two main reasons: (1) past abuses automatically invalidate indulgences (dirty hands destroy the diamond), or (2) forensic holiness implies no remaining debt of temporal punishment or purification is required at death.

Indulgences are often misunderstood, ignored by Catholics in the pews, and rarely discussed from the pulpit. The Council of Trent raised indulgences to a dogma of the Catholic Church in 1563, but the application of indulgences began much earlier. (The history of indulgences is treated separately in Chapter 9.)

After Vatican II, some ecumenically focused Christian groups hoped indulgences would somehow disappear since the practice was optional and a source of division between Catholics and Protestants. However, that did not happen. Pope John Paul II, Pope Benedict XVI, and Pope Francis have all encouraged indulgences during their pontificates.[267]

Karl Rahner, an influential Catholic theologian in the 20th century, believed that "only a more profound doctrine about temporal punishment can offer any prospect of our being able to break down ... the objections and prejudices of Protestant and Eastern Christians against the Catholic teaching on punishment due to sin, [works of] satisfaction, and indulgences."[268]

Basics of Indulgences

Indulgences don't forgive sin, replace the Sacrament of Reconciliation, impact salvation, or remove the guilt of sin. The Church teaches that indulgences relieve some or all of the debt of temporal punishment due to sin for a soul in purgatory.

Formally, an indulgence is a partial or total remission of the temporal punishment due to sins whose guilt before God has already been forgiven, usually through the Sacrament of Reconciliation, for a soul in purgatory. In a state of grace (no unconfessed mortal sin), Christians can gain indulgences only under certain prescribed conditions specified by the Church's authority. The source of indulgences derives from the merits of Christ's life, passion, death, and resurrection and the pleasing satisfactions of the saints in heaven while on earth.[269] Indulgences may be gained for oneself to be used after death, earned for other souls in purgatory, or given to God to use as he pleases.

The total remission of temporal punishment is called a *plenary indulgence* and requires complete detachment from all sin (even venial) when gained.[270] To receive a plenary indulgence, the individual must additionally make a sacramental confession, receive Holy Communion, and pray for the pope's intentions a few days before or after the specified pious act.

Only God knows if an individual receives an indulgence or how efficacious it is because the recipient must possess a sincere conversion of heart and union with God.[271] Thus, performing certain outward signs is *insufficient* to gain an indulgence. Through indulgences, the Church petitions God to accept the works of satisfaction (associated with indulgences) to mitigate or shorten the sufferings of the souls in purgatory. Indulgences in the Church's contemporary understanding are a move to emphasize Christ's mercy.

The power to grant indulgences is restricted to the pope or his temporary designee.[272] The Church claims the pope's authority from the "keys of the office" that Christ "handed" to Peter (cf. Mt 16:19) and from the power to forgive sins (cf. Jn 20:23) that Jesus passed to his apostles.[273] In 1967, Pope Paul VI wrote that the pastors of the Church [referring to the popes] "could set the individual free from the vestiges of sins by applying the merits of Christ and of the saints led gradually, in the course of the centuries and under the influence of the Holy Spirit's continuous inspiration of the people of God, to the usage of indulgences which represented a progression in the doctrine and discipline of the Church rather than a change."[274]

Indulgences are an extension of the Church's historic role in prescribing penances (works of satisfaction or temporal penalties) for confessed sin through the Sacrament of Reconciliation. However, through indulgences, the Church withdraws those temporal penalties in the afterlife for (venial or confessed and forgiven mortal) sins committed in this life.

The Church teaches that the Sacrament of Reconciliation removes the eternal punishment due to sin and potentially a part of the temporal punishment (depending on the penance and penitent). Indulgences are complementary to a partial effect of Reconciliation in that indulgences remove part or all of the temporal punishment due to sin.

Rahner defended the Church's power to commute "sentences" in the afterlife. He noted that the Sacrament of Reconciliation removes the guilt of sin before God by a juridical act of the Church through the action of the Holy Spirit conferred by Holy Orders. The priest acts in the person of Christ (*persona Christi*) by the power of the Holy Spirit. The penance, assigned by the priest and performed by the penitent, removes some, but not all, of the temporal consequences of sin. Rahner asserts that it is harder to remove the guilt of sin before God (through the Sacrament of Reconciliation) than the temporal punishment due to sin (via indulgences). And that if the Church can do the lesser, she can do the greater.[275]

Holy cards printed before 1976 often contained a prayer on the back, listing a number of indulged days earned for a soul in purgatory by praying the prayer. In 1976, Pope Paul VI did away with the days of indulgences and reduced the remaining indulgenced prayers and works to the most important prayers and works of piety, charity, and penance.[276] The number of days designation harkened back to the early Church's penitential discipline when public penances could take years to complete before the penitent was readmitted to the full sacramental and community life in the Church. Sometimes, the penitent would die before completing his assigned penance, which led to the community assuming part of his penance.[277]

The Church's dogma of indulgences rests on two other teachings: the *Communion of Saints* and the *Treasury of the Church,* addressed below.

Communion of Saints

The *Communion of Saints*, also called the Mystical Body of Christ, includes the saints in heaven, those in purgatory, and the redeemed still on earth. The phrase "Communion of Saints" has been used since the 4th century.[278] The *Catechism* explains that the spiritual connection between its members is not destroyed by death:

In the communion of saints, "a perennial link of charity exists between the faithful who have already reached their heavenly home, those who are expiating their sins in purgatory, and those who are still pilgrims on earth. Between them there is, too, an abundant exchange of all good things." In this wonderful exchange, the holiness of one profits others well beyond the harm that the sin of one could cause others. Thus, recourse to the communion of saints lets the contrite sinner be more promptly and efficaciously purified of the punishments for sin.[279]

Until the Protestant Reformation, all Christians believed and took comfort that death did not destroy the bonds uniting those on earth to their beloved deceased. Asking the martyrs for their intercession (prayers) was considered especially efficacious by virtue of their martyrdom.

After the Reformation, many Protestant denominations adopted the phrase "Body of Christ" instead of "Communion of Saints" to denote the living who believed in Christ. The new terminology diminished the intercessory role of the saints in heaven and denied the intermediate state of purgatory.

Treasury of the Church

The source of indulgences is God's grace, drawn from the infinite merits of his Son and the pleasing merits of his saints while on earth and now in heaven. In his 1967 *Indulgentiarum Doctrina*, Pope Paul VI explained that the *Treasury of the Church* is not an accumulation of material wealth gathered over centuries. Instead, the wellspring consists of the 1) "infinite and inexhaustible value the expiation and the merits of Christ Our Lord have before God," and the 2) "truly immense, unfathomable and ever pristine value before God of the prayers and good works of the Blessed Virgin Mary and all the saints,

... [who] while attaining their own salvation ... cooperated in the salvation of their brothers in the unity of the Mystical Body."[280]

In 1999, Pope John Paul II wrote that indulgences express "the Church's full confidence of being heard by the Father when—in view of Christ's merits and, by his gift, those of Our Lady and the saints ... [the Church] asks him [God] to mitigate or cancel the painful aspect of punishment by fostering its medicinal aspect through other channels of grace [that is, indulgences]."[281]

Further Reflections and Open Questions

In this section, we ponder the relationship of indulgences to the function of purgatory and the implications of plenary indulgences.

Indulgences and Models of Purgatory

Scholar Martin Jugie, S.J. (1878-1954), accepted indulgences but felt their efficacy argued for a *Satisfaction Model* of purgatory. He wrote that indulgences, prayers, and Masses for the dead could hardly help purify the soul. Instead, he saw those practices as substitutionary or making up for a lack in the individual's suffrages while on earth for their sins.[282]

Although Jugie makes a good point, perhaps a counterpoint exists if we reflect on how we attempt to work through difficulties in this life. During hard times, we naturally seek the love and support of our family and closest friends, requesting prayers to God for clarity, strength, and guidance. We enlist the help of therapists, doctors, and spiritual counselors to help us find healing. Could it be possible that indulgences (and prayers and Masses) for souls in purgatory mitigate, in some sense, the temporal punishment due to sin by surrounding the souls with love and encouragement as they set about the process of sanctification, permitting nothing to come between God and the soul?

Here, we understand sanctification in purgatory as the difficult and painful process of character maturation. This includes detachment from the lies to which we have stubbornly clung in order to deny our sins and the harm we have caused to others and the world by our choices—now all laid bare after seeing the truth of our life's choices through the eyes of Christ. With the aid of indulgences, we can imagine the "painful integration" of one's entire life, viewed through the eyes of Christ, "taken under the grace of God" and happening "more quickly and intensively and therefore also less painfully. That this is possible can be seen in our life on this earth. Thus, depending on circumstances, aids offered, etc., the same living 'process of working out' a moral problem can proceed easily and quickly or painfully and slowly."[283]

While we cannot understand the mystery of how God makes us ready for heaven, we know something of love and forgiveness and our desire to remain connected to those we love. Indulgences may keep this connection open in a very encouraging way when the soul needs it most.

Plenary Indulgences and Instantaneous Sanctification

Philosopher Neil Judisch writes that through the mystical union of Christ and his faithful believers, along with intercessory prayer, the living can "assist the souls in Purgatory by advancing the *sanctification* in nonstandard, ecclesiastically sanctioned ways [i.e., indulgences], but nonetheless in ways that do not differ in kind from praying for them."[284] Judisch also asserted that the Satisfaction and Sanctification Models of purgatory are the same if properly understood.

Assuming Judisch's position, we may ask whether the two functions of purgatory: a) the expiation of the temporal punishment due to sin and b) the purification functions of purgatory are *effectually equivalent*. If purgatory's satisfaction and sanctifying aspects are only *intellectually but not functionally separable*, what happens when a plenary indulgence removes all temporal punishment due to sin? Does this plenary indulgence translate the soul to perfection, given that the debt of temporal punishment has been fully satisfied?

The *Catechism* is judiciously terse, saying only that purification on earth or in purgatory frees one from the temporal punishment of sin.[285] If functionally equivalent, we wonder if a plenary indulgence differs from God perfecting the soul in the "twinkling of an eye" when a plenary indulgence fully commutes the soul's debt of temporal punishment. In the Church's parlance of indulgences, could we not then reformulate the Protestant theology of forensic justification (instantaneous holiness imputed at death) to mean that saving faith in Jesus Christ (*sola fides*) is tantamount to a plenary indulgence?[286]

The Church does not say how indulgences work in the hands of God. We know the eternal time of God is ever-present. Time after death is not chronological as we know and experience it in this life. Hence, what "twinkling of an eye" means in eternity is unknown. If we are honest, the temporal punishment and purification functions of purgatory are as mysterious as they are helpful to understanding how God's justice and mercy operate in tandem in purgatory. Christianity is God's attempt to reach man, while theology is our attempt to understand what this might mean. The Church provides dogmatic teachings to keep us on the right path, but much remains mysterious and unknown even within the constraints of dogma. The redeemed shall have eternity to worship and contemplate the mystery and wonder of God.

If indulgences cancel the painful aspects of the soul's rehabilitation, would we not desire our friends and family to offer indulgences for us when we die? Nowadays, we cannot assume they will or that they will even know what an indulgence is.[287]

Summary Points

Several points are worth summarizing before we next turn to the "messy" history of indulgences:

1. "An indulgence is a remission before God of the temporal punishment for sins, whose guilt is forgiven, which a properly disposed member of the Christian faithful obtains under certain and clearly defined conditions through the intervention of the Church, which, as the minister of Redemption, dispenses and applies authoritatively the treasury of the expiatory works of Christ and the saints."[288]
2. The *Communion of the Saints* is the union of all the redeemed, living and dead, united through Christ in love. This fraternal charity motivates the exchange of spiritual "goods" in indulgences.
3. The source of indulgences is called the infinite *Treasury of the Church*, which consists of Christ's infinite merits and the merits of the saints in heaven who have pleased God while on earth.
4. Only the pope or his temporary designee, acting with the pope's

authority, can approve indulgences (prayers and actions, whether partial or plenary).[289]
5. The Church lists indulged grants, actions, and prayers in its *Manual of Indulgences (Enchiridion Indulgentiarum)*.[290]
6. Even if an individual performs specified indulged actions, prayers, or devotions listed in the *Manual of Indulgences*, only God knows if an indulgence is granted to an individual.
7. Earning a plenary indulgence requires that the individual be free from mortal sin, receive the Sacraments of Reconciliation and the Eucharist, and pray for the pope's intentions (with specific prayers) within several days of performing the indulged work associated with the *plenary indulgence*.

In the next chapter, we examine the historical evolution of indulgences [including the theological development of the *Communion of the Saints* and the *Treasury (of Merits) of the Church*], how the abuse of indulgences by some unscrupulous individuals ignited the Protestant Reformation (and the rejection of purgatory) and the much-needed Catholic Counter-Reformation,[291] and, ultimately, the dogmatic assertion of indulgences by the Church.

9 – THE HISTORY OF INDULGENCES

Unfortunately, the practice of indulgences has at times been improperly used ... by which the power of the keys was humiliated and penitential satisfaction weakened, or through the collection of 'illicit profits' by which indulgences were blasphemously defamed.[292]
Pope Paul VI

The Catholic Church's teaching on indulgences is not simple. Grasping the prerequisite concepts requires some theological sophistication. The history of indulgences is no less complex, perhaps more so. The precursor of indulgences is present in the penitential rites of the early Church. Muslim expansionism and the Crusades further catalyzed the development of indulgences. The Scholastics provided the theological foundation for indulgences to refine papal praxis to eventual dogma. The Protestant Reformation provided the impetus to elevate the Church's teaching on indulgences during the Council of Trent to the doctrine we find today in the *Catechism of the Catholic Church*.

Connection to Penitential Rites

Indulgences evolved and spread gradually from penitential rites by the end of the 3rd century, as evidenced in the writing of St. Cyprian, Bishop of Carthage (249-258). As noted in Chapter 7, Cyprian had wrestled with the pastoral issue of bringing the *lapsi* (lapsed Christians) back into communion with the Church after the persecution of Decian (249-251). When threatened with torture or death, the *lapsi* had offered sacrifice to Roman gods or had convinced the Roman authorities, using forged documentation, that they had.

When the persecution ended, Cyprian took a merciful stance against the rigorists, who felt the *lapsi* (deemed guilty of apostasy) should not be allowed back into the Church. However, Cyprian let the *lapsi* back in but insisted on long, rigorous penances, which were the norm for sins such as apostasy, fornication, adultery, abortion, and murder. Under Decian's persecution, the sufferings of martyrs, who had died for their Christian faith, and the *confessors*, who had remained true to their faith and had survived torture, were "credited with the power of compensating [for] the sin of the *lapsi*."[293] By the heavenly intercession of martyrs and earthly prayers of the confessors, the penitential discipline of the *lapsi*, who were in danger of death and unable to complete their penance, drew upon the martyrs' merits and the confessors' works.

In his letter *De Lapsi*, Cyprian references the "heavenly crowns of the martyrs, [the] … spiritual triumphs of the confessors,"[294] and "the power which the *merits* of the martyrs and the *works* of the just have with the Judge [Christ]."[295] He wrote that God "can show clemency and forgive; He can take into account what the martyrs have asked for on their [the *lapsi's*] behalf and what the bishops have done for them."[296]

Three centuries later, in a sermon of St. Ceasarius of Arles (d. 542), we learn of a sinner who elected the option for public confession over private confession because he sought the whole Christian community's help to make reparation for his sins. Ceasarius wrote, "Considering the number of his sins, he sees that he is incapable of himself alone to make satisfaction for such grave evils; and … is anxious to seek out the assistance of the whole people."[297] Through Ceasarius's sermon, the sinner enlists and requests the help of the living to offer penance for the punishment due to sin. Similarly, Cyprian's letter suggests "borrowing" from the merits of the suffering of the living (i.e., confessors) and the dead (i.e., martyrs).[298]

By the 10th century, private auricular confession assumed its modern form. From the 10th century forward, the penitent could reduce ecclesial assigned penances for confessed sins by charitable works and almsgiving, creating a fluid transition to the holy-war-crusade indulgences.

During the 11th and 12th centuries, the words *absolutio, relaxatio, remissio, venia, condonatio,* and *indulgentia* were used to indicate a partial or total remission of penance due to sacramental confession, but also for the other extra-sacramental actions, such as indulgences.[299] This dual usage has resulted in confusion among secular historians.

Indulgences and the "Holy Wars"

The antecedents of indulgences (or proto-indulgences)[300] were developed alongside European feudalism beginning in the early Middle Ages (c.500-c.1050), were institutionalized in the High Middle Ages (c.1050-c.1300), and were dogmatized shortly after the late Middle Ages (c.1300-c.1500) during the last session of the Council of Trent (1563). The medieval period, spanning the entire Middle Ages, is known as the "Age of Faith" because, during this time, the Church was integrated into the very fabric of civil and religious life.

Because the separation of Church and State has been "hallowed" since the Age of Reason (c.1685-c.1815), the control exercised by the medieval Church in all matters of daily life may sound quite oppressive to us. However, this oversimplification is unschooled in the realities of the Middle Ages and the Church's role in protecting and ordering life during this time. The power and influence of the Church during the Middle Ages led to some of the darkest periods in Church history but also to some of its highest intellectual, artistic, and social achievements, including establishing hospitals and universities and caring for the poor.

Islamic incursion into traditionally Christian lands and the Levant further contributed to the development of indulgences. As early as the 9th century, regional armies were formed, with the papal rewards of forgiveness of sins, to defend against Muslim invasions. "The recognition that 'fighting for Christ and the Church was meritorious in the sight of God, and ... worthy of a spiritual reward proclaimed by the Church' was not something [new] that Pope Urban II first brought about"[301] when he offered what history books traditionally call the first "holy war" indulgence.

There were many worldly reasons why a medieval man would join a "holy war" besides the spiritual benefits of a plenary indulgence. Historian Will Durant explains that besides those "sincerely religious souls desiring to rescue the land of Christ's birth and death," serfs and prisoners could attain their freedom; for others, taxation stopped, and debts were canceled.[302] In addition to the "thousands of vagrants," were men who were "tired of hopeless poverty, adventurers ready for brave enterprise, younger sons hoping to carve out fiefs for themselves in the East, merchants seeking new markets for their goods, knights whose enlisting serfs had left them laborless."[303]

Well before the First Crusade (1096–1099), Popes Leo IV (847-855), John VIII (872-882), and Alexander II (1061-1063) had promised eternal life (by complete forgiveness of sins) to Christian warriors who died bravely fighting the Muslims. These spiritual rewards restored the slain warrior to a state of innocence as if a second Baptism. These papal-bestowed proto-indulgences achieved additional specificity over time.

In 853, after Muslim invaders sacked the Basilica of St. Peter, Pope Leo IV assured prospective Frankish warriors of eternal salvation if they died in battle while coming to the defense of Christendom:

[T]he kingdom of heaven will be given as a reward to those who shall be killed in this war. For the Omnipotent knows that they lost their lives fighting for the truth of the faith, for the preservation of their country, and the defense of Christians.[304]

In 878, Pope John VIII (872-82) addressed a formal letter (or Papal Bull) to the bishops in France stating the required conditions to gain the *indulgentiam* (proto-indulgence). John VIII defended his authority to forgive the fallen warrior's sins and assure them of eternal life. John VIII incentivized Christian men to perform a specific good work (defending the Church and preserving Christianity) under the conditions prespecified by the Church (because of their love of their Catholic faith and dying bravely). If the fallen warrior met all requirements, he would be released entirely from his sins and gain eternal life:

[T]hose who have recently died in war, fighting in defense of the Holy Church of God and for the preservation of the Christian religion and of the state, or those who may in the future fall in the same cause, may obtain indulgence for their sins (indulgentiam ... delictorum). We confidently reply that those who, out of love of the Catholic religion, shall die in battle fighting bravely against pagans and unbelievers, shall enter the rest of eternal life. ... We ... absolve their sins ... by the intercession

of St. Peter the Apostle, who has the power of binding and loosing in heaven and on earth (Matt. 16:19), and commend them by our prayers to the Lord.[305]

Prompted by the Morish invasion of Spain and addressed to the clergy in Volturara Appula (southeastern Italy), Pope Alexander II issued a proto-indulgence in 1063. He stated that the spiritual benefit removed the *penance* for *confessed* sin.

We urge with paternal charity that those who are determined to set out for Spain think with maximum care about what they, divinely inspired, have decided to carry out. Let a measure of penance be imposed on each and every one of them who shall confess, according to the quality of his sins, to his bishop or spiritual father, so that the devil may not accuse them of impenitence. We, accompanying [them] with prayer, by the authority of the holy apostles Peter and Paul, [thereby] lift their penance and give them remission of sins.[306]

Thirty-two years later, in 1095, during the Council of Claremont, Pope Urban II initiated the First Crusade. He called for the rescue of Christians in the East and the taking back of Jerusalem from the Seljuk Turks. He granted the following indulgence:

Whoever for devotion alone, and not for the purpose of gaining honor or money, heads for Jerusalem to liberate the Church of God, that expedition is to be imputed to him [as satisfaction] *for all penance.*[307]

Urban II's indulgence of 1095 is usually cited by secular historians as the *first* indulgence granted by the Church, ignoring the previous proto-indulgences granted by Leo IV, John VIII, and Alexander II. According to historian Paul Chevedden, there was little difference between the 1095 indulgence of Urban II and the earlier proto-indulgences.[308]

Under Pope Innocent III (1161-1216), the Church was at the zenith of its *influence*: politically, socially, intellectually, and spiritually. The Church used alms to help pay for the Crusades and building projects, including hospitals, churches, and cathedrals. In England, hospitals relied almost entirely on alms by the 11th century.[309]

The Second Council of Lyons (1274), convened under Pope Gregory X (1271-1276), granted an indulgence for participation in the Seventh Crusade. The Pope invoked the power of the keys, offering participant warriors "full pardon for their sins about which they are truly and heartily contrite and have spoken in confession" with the requirement that those fighting have as their intention to aid the Holy Land by "recompensing of the just" [i.e., freeing the Christians from Muslim oppression]; and to those who offered material help, the Pope offered a "share in this remission, according to the nature of their help and the intensity of their devotion."[310]

The popes claimed the Church's authority to grant indulgences by apostolic authority in two ways. The first was by the "power of the keys" that Jesus gave to Peter and passed onto each successive pope. The second was by the power to hold and loose sins given to the twelve and passed on to the other "presbyters" by the laying on of hands (the bishops and those they installed as priests through Holy Orders).

In summary, indulgences were granted for the remission of the penance of sin for the penitent only and *exclusively* connected to his *canonical penance*.[311] The Church had yet to extend the application beyond the recipient of the indulgence to other souls in purgatory, such as a deceased family member, that would happen shortly after the Eighth Crusade at the end of the 13th century.

Scholastic Clarifications (13th-14th Century)

Several theological points begged clarification before the Church would dogmatically confirm indulgences. The Scholastic school of thought supplied the missing systematization and provided answers to the implicit theological questions surrounding indulgences. The motivation (or *why*) of indulgences was identified as the charity abounding within the *Communion of Saints*; their source (or *how*) was to be found within the *Treasury (of Merits) of the Church*.

Within the universities, the Scholastics debated and hammered out concepts critical to both indulgences and purgatory, such as temporal punishment due to sin in the afterlife. Franciscan St. Bonaventure (1221-1274), among others, defended the "power over purgatory of the Church in general and the pope in particular."[312] St. Thomas Aquinas (1225-1274) was the most famous of the Scholastics, greatly influencing Catholic doctrine in many areas, including temporal punishment for sin, indulgences, and purgatory.

By the Second Council of Lyons (1274), the Scholastic theologians, most notably Aquinas in his *Summa Theologica*, had worked out the concept of "debt of temporal punishment" due to sins. Aquinas defended the Church's practice of granting indulgences and their power, but only under certain conditions:

> *[I]ndulgences have precisely the efficacy claimed for them, provided that he who grants them have the authority, that the recipient have charity, and that, as regards the cause, there be piety which includes the honor of God and the profit of our neighbor.*[313]

The *Treasury of Merits of the Church,* which at some point transitioned to being called the *Treasury of the Church,* was first suggested around 1230 by Hugh of St-Cher, a Dominican friar, scholar, and cardinal.[314] St. Thomas Aquinas and St. Albert the Great (c.1200 - 1280) further expounded on this "treasury."

The phrase "Treasury of Merits" is found in the 1343 Papal Bull *Unigenitus Dei Filius* by Pope Clement VI. He explains that the *Treasury of Merits* comes first and foremost from Christ's redemptive work, and then in the spirit of Colossians 1:24, Clement VI writes that the merits of Mary and the saints (the elect), while on earth and now in heaven, add to the treasure. He cites the keys of Peter as the source of the Church's authority to dispense of the *Treasury of Merits* for the relief of temporal punishment due to sins:

> *Therefore, how great a treasure did the good Father* [God] *acquire from this* [Christ's redeeming death on the cross] *for the Church militant* [the faithful on earth]*, so that the mercy of so great an effusion was not rendered useless, vain or superfluous, wishing to lay up treasures for His* [God's] *sons, so that thus the Church is an infinite treasure to men, so that they who use it, become the friends of God.* (Wis. 7:14)

> *Indeed this treasure ... through blessed Peter, the keeper of the keys of heaven and his successors, his vicars on earth, He* [God]*, through the Church] has committed to be dispensed for the good of the faithful, both from proper and reasonable causes, now for the whole, now for partial remission of temporal punishment due to sins, in general as in particular (according as they know to be expedient with God), to be applied mercifully to those who truly repentant have confessed.*

> *Indeed, to the mass of this treasure the merits of the Blessed Mother of God and of all the elect* [saints in heaven] *from the first just even to the last, are known to give their help; concerning the consumption or the diminution of this be there should no fear at any time, because of the infinite merits of Christ ... [and] that the more are brought to justification by its application, the greater is the increase of the merits themselves.*[315]

Post-Crusades

The Crusades were over by the end of the 13th century. By then, it was commonplace for popes to grant plenary indulgences for various pious acts, such as making pilgrimages and almsgiving. The Church had used alms to fund the latter Crusades, construct magnificent cathedrals, and build churches, hospitals, and schools to benefit everyone independent of the battlefield.[316] In 1351, Pope Clement VI confirmed the nature of these indulgences and their conditions for being granted in a personal letter to the patriarch of the Armenian Orthodox Christians.

The Roman Pontiff alone is able to establish sacred general canons, to grant plenary indulgences to those who visit the thresholds of the Apostles, Peter and Paul, or to those who go to the Holy Land, or to any of the faithful who are truly and fully repentant and have confessed.[317]

Once the popes opened the door to broader almsgiving to receive indulgences, the twofold possibility of abuse entered. The alms might be considered a payment for the indulgence, thus losing sight of the conditions required to earn an indulgence—a deep conversion of heart and heartfelt contrition for sins.[318] Also, "those [popes] who granted indulgences might be tempted to make them a means of raising money: and, even where the rulers of the Church were free from blame in this matter, there was room for corruption in their officials and agents, or among the popular preachers of indulgences."[319] And to be clear, there were deplorable abuses, some quite serious.[320]

Against this backdrop, Pope Boniface VIII (1294-1303), whose pontificate is considered by some as starting a downward spiral in the Church,[321] granted indulgences for pilgrimages to the Basilica of St. Peter. In his Jubilee Bull *Antiquorum Habet*, Boniface VIII wrote that the "ancients" believed that "those approaching the honorable Basilica of the Prince of the Apostles are granted great remissions of sins and indulgences. We ... confirm and by apostolic authority approve all such remissions and indulgences, holding them all and individually valid and pleasing [.]"[322]

Extension of Personal Indulgence to Souls in Purgatory

In 1476, Pope Sixtus IV affirmed that indulgences were efficacious for those in purgatory, drawing from the *Treasury of the Church*. He granted a "plenary remission of punishments" where the almsgiver had the intention of helping souls "exposed to purgatorial fire for the expiation of punishments due them according to divine justice" who had given a "sum of money" toward the repair of the "church of Xancto."[323] In the same document, he emphasized that the Roman Pontiff had the power to remit the punishment of purgatory.

St. Peter's Basilica was also in great disrepair, having sustained damage from 9th-century Saracen raids and the ravages of time. Pope Julius II (1503-13) decided to demolish and rebuild the basilica and decreed that anyone who went to Confession, received Holy Communion, and then donated alms according to their means could receive a plenary indulgence.[324]

Pope Leo X continued this indulgence when, in 1517 (and again in 1518), he offered indulgences for those who gave alms to rebuild St. Peter's Basilica. He defended papal authority to grant indulgences by the power of the keys of St. Peter and connected indulgences to the remission of the temporal punishment due to confessed sins.

Leo X wrote a personal letter to the papal legate, Dominican Thomas Cajetan, in Germany. The letter reaffirmed that indulgences drew upon "the superabundant merits of Christ and the saints [*Treasury of the Church*] to these same faithful of Christ, who belong to Christ by the charity that joins the members [*Communion of Saints*], whether they be in this life or purgatory."[325]

Problems, Abuses, and Attempted Reforms

Indulgences grew in popularity during the High Middle Ages as a way to mitigate the suffering of beloved family members in purgatory. Around the 13th century, questors and pardoners helped the Church manage the logistics of granting indulgences. Questors, typically clergy, were allowed to preach about indulgences, whereas pardoners, typically laymen, were not. The pardoner was restricted to collecting alms for indulgences and then providing documentation for presentation to the priest at the time of the almsgiver's confession. Chaucer's *Canterbury Tales* made the role of pardoner and the potential for corruption infamous and fueled the still common perception of universal abuse.

In 1517, the year before Pope Leo X wrote his letter to Cajetan cited above, Martin Luther had posted his *Ninety-Five Thesis* in Whittenburg, Germany. (Martin Luther's actions likely motivated Leo X's letter to Cajetan.) Luther had been greatly disturbed by how indulgences were being represented and promoted. He also felt that the pope had no authority to intervene in the state of punishment of those in purgatory, which puts Pope Leo X's letter in context.

The popular narrative is that abuse was prevalent in granting and distributing indulgences. The scholarship over the last century does not support that charge in England. Such a view "may be challenged and revised in light of other evidence, such as the bishops' registers and pastoral manuals. When taken together, these sources indicate that church authorities monitored the pardoners imperfectly, but in the main, effectively, and therefore suggest that the damage the pardoners brought on the late medieval English church has been exaggerated."[326]

Even before the last Crusade, the Church had tried to rail in abuses associated with indulgences. In 1215, the Lateran Council under Pope Innocent III reprimanded bishops, in Canon 62, for promising partial indulgences beyond what the pope had approved:

Since, through indiscreet and superfluous indulgences which some prelates of churches do not hesitate to grant, contempt is brought on the keys of the Church, and the penitential discipline is weakened, we decree that on the occasion of the dedication of a church an indulgence of not more than one year be granted, whether it be dedicated by one bishop only or by many, and on the anniversary of the dedication the remission granted for penances enjoined is not to exceed forty days. We command also that in each case this number of days be made the rule in issuing letters of indulgences which are granted from time to time, since the Roman pontiff who possesses the plenitude of power customarily observes this rule in such matters.[327]

Canon 62 was reaffirmed in 1298 by Pope Boniface VIII's *Indulgentiae* and then again in 1313 by Pope Clement V's *Abusionibus*, which stated that the pardoner could not dispense vows, forgive sins, cancel penances already enjoined, or make claims that "whoever gives them alms frees the souls of three or more parents and friends from Purgatory and gains them entrance to Paradise."[328]

For over three centuries, popes had sought to minimize

overreaching and fraudulent behaviors of questors and pardoners and provide proper instruction through papal decrees and parish manuals without complete success. Moreover, the Black Death (1346-1352) had left the clergy decimated in Europe, further deteriorating the quality of priests.[329] The Council of Trent sought reforms to educate and better prepare men for the priesthood. Seminaries were created, but sadly, not until the Protestant Reformation was underway.

Eventually, during the Twenty-First Session of the Council of Trent (1562), the office of the questor was abolished, citing the "great scandal" and "depravity" caused by the "pernicious abuses of questors" that were "beyond of hope of amendment."[330] In the Twenty-Fifth Session (1567), Pope Pius V outlawed the collection of alms related to all indulgences due to the potential for abuse.[331]

To say that there has never been any abuse associated with this process granting indulgences by some unscrupulous individuals would be foolish.[332] In 1967, Pope Paul VI said as much in his Apostolic Constitution *Indulgentiarum Doctrina*, yet defended the proper uses of indulgences: "*[T]he Church, in deploring and correcting these improper uses 'teaches and establishes that the use of indulgences must be preserved because it is supremely salutary for the Christian people and authoritatively approved by the sacred councils[.]'*"[333]

The resulting abuse of indulgences, whether rare or rampant in the aggregate, ultimately led to the splintering of Christendom into many Protestant sects united primarily by their dislike of Catholicism but divided in their own theology and religious practices. As the Reformation's ideas spread, religion and politics became increasingly intertwined. Political support played a crucial role in the spread of the Reformation. And the behavior of certain questors and pardoners fueled subsequent controversy.

Protestant Reformation and the Declaration of Dogma

In the fall of 1517, Martin Luther (1493-1546) posted his infamous *Ninety-five Theses* on a church door in Wittenberg, Germany, where community notices were often posted. Martin Luther's eventual rejection of purgatory began with his repudiation of the abuses associated with indulgences.[334]

Luther's *Ninety-Five Theses* retained most aspects of the true doctrine of the Church. But in a fairly short time, according to theologian Philip Goyret, "the nucleus of the debate [started by Luther] shifted from the theology of indulgences to the theology of the Church," which included purgatory.[335] Goyret makes an important but often ignored distinction between the "first Luther" (still loyal to the doctrines of the Church), the "second Luther" (who rejected many doctrines of the Church, including purgatory), and the eventual, more pervasive, theological deviation that developed into Lutheranism.

Luther maintained that the power of indulgences came from prayers of the Church for the deceased [i.e., intercession] rather than the *Treasury of the Church* because he believed that neither the pope nor the Church had any power over the souls in purgatory. He wrote, "The pope does well when he grants remission to souls [in purgatory], not by the power of the keys (which he does not possess), but by way of intercession." [336]

Luther had formulated his theology of *sola fide, sola Scriptura, solus Christus, sola gratia* by 1521.[337] In 1537, he wrote that "purgatory, and every solemnity, rite, and commerce connected with it, is to be regarded as nothing but a specter of the devil."[338] Luther softens his extreme language later in the same document, stating that even if purgatory were neither "error nor idolatry," it would be best to abandon it because purgatory was "hopelessly bound up with unacceptable practices," such as indulgences.[339] Primarily, Luther's issues with purgatory were: purgatory is not found in Scripture, owing satisfaction for one's sins undercuts the sufficiency of Christ's redemptive work, and that God works the transformation to perfect holiness through our death as in a moment through the death and resurrection of Christ.[340]

John Calvin (1509-1564) described purgatory as a "horrid blasphemy" and "a deadly device of Satan; that it makes void the cross of Christ; that it offers intolerable insult to the divine mercy; that it undermines and overthrows our faith."[341] Calvin rejected the *Treasury of the Church* as the source of indulgences, insisting that such explanations substitute the blood of the martyrs for that of Christ.[342]

During the last session of the Council of Trent (1563), the Council deplored the corruption and evil practices associated with indulgences. The Council, however, reaffirmed their validity, its power to grant, and their efficacy:

> Since the power of granting indulgences was conferred by Christ on the Church, and she has made use of such power divinely given to her, even in the earliest times, the holy Synod teaches and commands that the use of indulgences, most salutary to a Christian people and approved by the authority of the sacred Councils, is to be retained in the Church, and it condemns those with anathema who assert that they are useless or deny that there is in the Church the power of granting them.[343]

By Calvin's time, the entire theology of purgatory had come under attack, inexorably linked to indulgences. It is no wonder that few Protestants of any denomination today are willing to take a second look at purgatory, given its close historical ties to indulgences. Discussions regarding purgatory can quickly devolve into the "sale of indulgences," which captures the nature of the abuses well but incorrectly extrapolates their abuse to 100% and misrepresents the Church's overall intent and dogma.

In the three paragraphs on purgatory found in the *Catechism of the Catholic Church*, the endorsement and efficacy of indulgences comprise the last. But it is still there, the very same as dogmatically proclaimed by the Council of Trent, although softer in tone.

Prayers for the Dead Revisited

Luther wrote that the power of indulgences came from the ability of the living to pray to God for the dead. In Luther's *Confession Concerning Christ's Supper* (1528), he wrote, "As for the dead, since Scripture gives us no information on the subject, I regard it as no sin to pray with free devotion in this or some similar fashion: 'Dear God, if this soul is in a condition accessible to mercy be thou gracious to it. And when this has been done once or twice, let it suffice.'"[344]

Other well-known Protestants, such as John Wesley, founder of the Methodist Church, thought it our duty to commend the souls of the dead to the care of God and hasten their ascent to glory.[345] C. S. Lewis prayed for the dead, recognizing that it is part of human nature to want to do so and somehow recognize that love's bonds survive death. "Of course, I pray for the dead. The action is so spontaneous, so all but inevitable, that only the most compulsive theological case against it would deter me. And I hardly know how the rest of my prayers would survive if those for the dead were forbidden."³⁴⁶

Some Protestant reformers objected to prayers for the dead. They mistakenly thought that Catholics believed their prayers removed the guilt of the deceased's sins and that prayers for the dead lessened the dependence on divine grace flowing from Christ's redeeming death, misplacing the emphasis on meritorious works.

In praying for the repose of the souls of those who precede us in death, Catholics commend them to the mercy of God. They ask that the saints in heaven—those closest to God—also extend charity toward the deceased with their prayers. Prayers for the dead by the living are essential to the *Communion of Saints* as understood by the Catholic Church. Pope Benedict XVI writes eloquently in *Spe Salvi* on this connection between the living and the dead. He reminds the faithful that it is never too late to pray for the dead, as the souls are outside time, and these acts of charity benefit the living as well as the dead.

> *Now a further question arises: if "Purgatory" is simply purification through fire in the encounter with the Lord, Judge and Savior, how can a third person intervene, even if he or she is particularly close to the other? When we ask such a question, we should recall that no man is an island, entire of itself. Our lives are involved with one another, through innumerable interactions they are linked together. No one lives alone. No one sins alone. No one is saved alone.*
>
> *The lives of others continually spill over into mine: in what I think, say, do and achieve. And conversely, my life spills over into that of others: for better and for worse. So my prayer for another is not something extraneous to that person, something external, not even after death. In the interconnectedness of Being, my gratitude to the other—my prayer for him—can play a small part in his purification.*
>
> *And for that there is no need to convert earthly time into God's time: in the communion of souls simple terrestrial time is superseded. It is never too late to touch the heart of another, nor is it ever in vain. In this way we further clarify an important element of the Christian concept of hope. Our hope is always essentially also hope for others; only thus is it truly hope for me too. As Christians we should never limit ourselves to asking: how can I save myself? We should also ask: what can I do in order that others may be saved and that for them too the star of hope may rise? Then I will have done my utmost for my own personal salvation as well.*³⁴⁷

Prayers for the dead have gone by the wayside with the "demise" of purgatory for most Protestants (and some Catholics, too), but even rejecting indulgences for theological reasons or due to past abuses does not logically repudiate the existence or the need for an intermediate state, like purgatory.

10 – CULTURAL EXPRESSIONS & PRETERNATURAL EXPERIENCES OF PURGATORY

[P]rivate revelations must be received with very great reserve. But it would be unreasonable to dismiss them all as fables[.] [348]
Martin Jugie, S.J.

The time period of our birth dramatically influences our ability to conceptualize, interpret, and communicate our thoughts, aspirations, and dreams. It informs our impressions of all things, including purgatory. We have the advantage of a long historical record to look back upon and the gift of literacy (which for many centuries was the domain of a privileged few). We have incredible access to educational resources unimaginable even a hundred years ago.

From our 21st-century vantage point, we can observe purgatory swinging between the poles of sanctification and satisfaction throughout its history. This oscillation is apparent in the written ecclesiastical record, literature, art, and legends of and writings of the saints. Yet, the dogma of the Catholic Church remains unchanged for purgatory, established first at the Council at Florence and reaffirmed a hundred years later at Trent in the 16th century, incorporating both elements of purification and expiation.

To some academic observers, such as philosopher Jerry Walls, the Church's model of purgatory swung to sanctification during "the twentieth century," and "today it is the primary if not the sole emphasis."[349] Yet others, such as philosopher Neal Judisch, argue convincingly that the Sanctification and Satisfaction Model are the same when properly understood,[350] forming what I call a Unified Model.

This chapter samples art, literature, and reported purgatorial experiences captured in writing by those who came before us—not popes or church councils—but laypersons and religious. Some are canonized saints, and some are not. Following this trail of cultural breadcrumbs, we observe the tension of purgatory, swinging between the poles of sanctification and satisfaction sprinkled liberally with the Catholic imagination.

Medieval Art

From the time of Pope Gregory the Great to the 19th century, images of purgatorial fires ignited by Augustine of Hippo burned in the imaginations of Christians. Throughout the Middle Ages, purgatory was often characterized as a place of torture and flames in literature and art as a kind of temporary hell. Yet, for some medieval mystics and saints (some we shall meet in this chapter), purgatory was envisioned as a place of hope and happiness while simultaneously a place of horrific pain.

Figure 1 displays a column miniature found in the *Missal of Eberhard von Greiffenklau* (c.1425-1450).[351] This *Missal*, a Roman Catholic prayerbook, used for following along during Mass, was created when bookmaking was still an art practiced exclusively by monks in monasteries. The monk-artist placed his illustration in the "Votive Masses" section, a liturgy for special occasions, including funerals.

The artist represented souls in purgatory undergoing postmortem cleansing and purgatorial punishments. Red flames, symbolizing purgatorial punishments, engulf the souls as they pray, "*Miserere mei, Deus: secundum magnam misericordiam tuam,*" translated as "Have mercy on me, O God: according to your great mercy."[352] As depicted, the souls are not writhing in pain or trying to escape; instead, with hands folded in prayer, they praise God for his mercy and "appear to bear this torment with humble resignation."[353]

This artistic interpretation of the Church's teaching on Purgatory was created around the time of the Council of Florence. That the Council of Trent, in its last session, dogmatically confirmed the Council of Florence's declarations on purgatory makes this image of particular interest.

Figure 1. *Souls in Purgatory (column miniature), Missal of Eberhard von Greiffenklau / (c. 1425-1450) / Masters of Zwder van Culemborg, The Walters Art Museum, Baltimore / CC0 1.0 Universal*

The painting shown in Figure 2 is different in scope than the column miniature of Figure 1. In this second image, Italian painter Lodovico Carracci (1555-1619) presents a visual "catechism" of the Church's teaching on indulgences, dogmatized by the Council of Trent during his lifetime. Created nearly two centuries later than the *Missal of Eberhard von Greiffenklau*, the flames of purgatory remain burning. The presence of Jesus, Mary, and Saints in heaven symbolizes the *Treasury of the Church*, the source of indulgences. The artist represents the efficacy of indulgences by the angel's upward-pointing index finger while lifting the chosen soul towards heaven.

Neither the Councils of Florence nor Trent referenced any fires of purgatory in their dogmatic statements. However, as Catholic priest J. P. Arendzen, D.D. (1873-1954) wrote, "For many centuries in the West in popular addresses to the faithful and in the popular imagination, both *fire* and *pain of the senses* have been taken for granted, but between this and official Catholic teaching there is a *wide margin* (emphasis added)."[354]

Figure 2. *A Fiery Purgatory (c. 1610) / Lodovico Carracci / Pinacoteca Art Gallery, Vatican / Public domain, via Wikimedia Commons.*

Medieval Literature

Today's most translated literary work, second only to the Bible, is Dante Alighieri's *Divine Comedy (Divina Commedia)*.[355] Dante's epic poem, completed in 1321, contains three parts: the *Inferno*, *Purgatorio*, and *Paradiso*. In it, Dante embarks on a spiritual journey as he comes to abhor sin and understand its consequences by visiting the three realms of the dead. With the semi-freedom of poetic license, he caricatured a version of purgatory emphasizing purification more than punishment, contrary to popular perception in his time.[356]

Dante's vision of purgatory resonated with the populace to a lasting effect, and according to agnostic historian Jacques Le Goff was the "noblest" representation of purgatory ever conceived by the mind of man" while "affirming the essence of dogma and leaving much to the sensibility and imaginations of individual Christians."[357] purgatory was seen by Dante as an opportunity "of unliving the life that we have lived, and building up for ourselves a past through which 'the stream of memory can flow unstained' ... of living ourselves out of the thing with which we have united ourselves and living ourselves into the thing we have severed ourselves from."[358]

Philosopher Jerry Walls suggests that due to Dante's influence as a poet and popular "theologian" during the Late Middle Ages, "a stronger stress on sanctification became apparent" as in *Purgatorio*, "but the element of satisfaction came to dominate after that, and later still became the exclusive emphasis in much Roman Catholic theology."[359]

Purgatory, as a place of sanctification, has always been more popular with the faithful and less terrifying. Yet even a hundred years ago, we see evidence of theologians "bumping" against each other with their differing models of purgatory.

Popular Opinions, Legends, and Stories

A 1922 article published in the *Irish Theological Journal* by M.F. Egan, S.J., documents the tension between the Satisfaction Model (popular among the theologians and clergy) and the Sanctification Model (desired by the people) in the early 20th century.

> *"There are two views concerning ... Purgatory. The first view* [a Sanctification Model] *is that which finds favour with the popular mind; the second* [a Satisfaction Model], *that which is the expression of strict theological truth. The popular mind about Purgatory is that one ends thereby gradually acquiring purity and saintliness, while the theological truth is that a man, not a reprobate at the hour of death, becomes a perfect saint the moment after, whatever be his debts to the divine justice, ...* [are] *paid to the last farthing."* [360]

Egan argued that there was value in both and that "the persistence after death of struggle and contradiction in the faithful but imperfect soul is in accord with St. Thomas's [Aquinas's] *psychological* doctrine (emphasis added)."[361]

For many faithful Catholics, especially before literacy was widespread in modern times, legends and stories of purgatorial visitors shaped their beliefs about purgatory. Even today, such stories pique our curiosity and command our attention, at least, if not more, than theological musings about purgatory.[362]

In 1893, François-Xavier Schouppe, S.J., wrote *Purgatory: Explained by the Lives and Legends of the Saints*, containing hundreds of stories and legends about purgatorial visions and visitations. He wrote this book to encourage his readers to (1) expiate their sins while on earth and (2) pray for the dead, who, upon release from purgatory, will pray for those who prayed for them. Schouppe proposes that only through a special grace of God can a soul in purgatory interact with the living.

Most of Schouppe's stories were originally recorded or preserved as oral legends by those in religious life, presumably with fervent orthodoxy and great sensitivity towards the dead. The sheer volume of stories is staggering and almost overwhelming. Some legends date to the 10th century, but most are from the late Middle Ages, plus or minus a century. The author writes that it is impossible to read these stories "without trembling" and that the fire of purgatory, which is "enkindled by Divine Justice," generates such "excruciating pain" that all the "penances of the saints, [and] all the suffering of the martyrs put together, are as nothing."[363]

Schouppe defines *visions* as "subjective lights, infused by God into the understanding of his creatures" to help them understand his mysteries, often occurring during ecstasy and appealing to the "eyes of the soul," not to be taken literally.[364] He defines *apparitions* as "objective phenomena" with a "real exterior object."[365]

In every case of apparitions, the purgatorial visitors requested suffrages or Masses for themselves and appeared in a state of great suffering, inspiring compassion. A common thread in such stories is that such apparitions and visions are unsettling and disturbing for the recipient.

Moving from legends and stories to artifacts, we find an interesting set of "specimens" in a small room in Rome's Church of the Sacred Heart of Suffrage. Fr. Victor Jouet (1839-1912) began this collection to encourage suffrages for the souls in purgatory among the faithful. Many items have been removed over time. The remaining burnt hand imprints and fingerprints have origins less likely to incur criticism.[366]

Writings of the Saints

Precisely because of the mysterious nature of life after death and natural human curiosity, there is much fascination with visionaries and mystics associated with purgatory. The detailed descriptions of purgatory and the appearance of souls begging for prayers and Masses fall into the category of *private revelation*, even for the visions reported by canonized saints.

The German mystic St. Gertrude the Great, OSB (1256-1302), is considered the patron saint of the souls in purgatory. Only one of her reputed works, *The Life and Revelations of Saint Gertrude*, survives. Most of the writing is attributed to other nuns in her community and was written after her death. Gertrude reported many visions of deceased religious sisters and brothers in purgatory, whose deliverance from purgatory was attributed to her prayers, suffrages, or Masses she had said for them. Her writings stress the efficacy of prayers for the dead to hasten the entry of souls into heaven. Gertrude's visions of souls in purgatory are consistent with fire and great suffering, even for minor sins. However, like her contemporary Dante, she also writes of the purifying nature of the suffering endured by the souls in purgatory.[367]

Laywoman St. Catherine of Genoa (1447-1510), often referred to as the "doctress of purgatory" (although not one of the four female Doctors of the Church), had many beautiful insights into purgatory. Her teachings have inspired individuals like St. Francis de Sales, St. Robert Bellarmine, Cardinal John Henry Newman, and many others.[368] Catherine's followers compiled her teachings in two books: *Treatise on Purgatory* and *The Spiritual Dialogue*. Unique for her time, but like Dante, Catherine captured the paradox of purgatory: a state of inexplicable joy, second only to heaven, and simultaneously a place of great suffering. In full accord with modern theologians, Catherine maintained that the soul's will in purgatory is perfectly aligned with the Divine Will and that the soul chooses purgatory to remove the rust of sin on its soul.

During the latter period of her life, Catherine became an administrator of a large hospital. Her reputation for extreme organization, sacrifice, and charity grew in this role. During her time at the hospital, she experienced a great spiritual awakening.[369] Her thoughts congealed, and her following grew. She wrote that in purgatory, God kindles a great fire in the soul to transform it back to its first state before sin.[370] For Catherine, purgatory was a great gift of divine mercy.

St. Teresa of Avila, OCD (1515-1582), was acquainted with St. Gertrude's book, as one of her confessors recommended it for her reading. Whether Gertrude's work influenced Teresa or not, their visions have many similarities, such as Jesus lifting souls from purgatory to heaven. Teresa was greatly devoted to praying for the souls in purgatory, as documented in her autobiography.[371] Teresa describes how the Lord allowed her to see the efficacy of her prayers (which were voluminous) for the release of souls from purgatory from their terrible suffering. She believed that her hardships in life, when patiently suffered, substituted for purgatory. "If I had trials, they would be meritorious; and if unhappiness, it would serve as purgatory if I accepted it in the service of God."[372]

St. Stanislaus Papczynski (1631-1701), the founder of the Congregation of Marian Fathers of the Immaculate Conception, had a great sensitivity and ministry to relieve the suffering of others. He encouraged prayers for the souls in purgatory, "especially the souls of soldiers who had died in battle and of the victims of pestilence."[373] Three visions of purgatory, one in which he entered into the horrific suffering of the souls, deepened his devotion.

Praying for the souls in purgatory was one of the primary charisms of the new congregation Papczynski founded, as it remains today. Papczyński did not preach "fire and brimstone"; instead, he encouraged everyone "to contemplate God's mercy," proclaiming "that God's heart is open to all," a charism evident in the Marian Fathers' ministry to inculcate devotion to "The Divine Mercy." Papczynski was noted for his "tender approach to sinners," and by analogy, Papczyński referred to the Blessed Mother as *"the hook"* catching sinners to bring them back to God."[374]

Two modern canonized saints: St. Pio of Pietrelcina (1887-1968), an Italian Capuchin monk also known as Padre Pio, and St. Faustina (1905-1938), a Polish sister of Our Lady of Mercy, were particularly devoted to the souls in purgatory. Each reported encounters (or apparitions) from the dead requesting suffrages to expedite the remainder of their purgation.

Padre Pio recounted the story of an old man who had startled Pio from his prayers in a locked room. "My name was Pietro DiMauro," said the man. "I died in this friary on Sep 18, 1908, in room No. 4, when this was still a poor house ... of burns and asphyxiation. I am still in Purgatory and have need of a Holy Mass to be freed. The Lord has permitted me to come to ask your assistance."[375] Padre Pio agreed to offer a Mass for him the next day.

Later, Pio, much disturbed by the event, shared the experience with a fellow monk, Padre Paolino, who, on the following day, verified with city hall that a person with the same name had perished thirty-two years earlier in a fire at the friary in the room when the building had been used to house the poor.

Those who reject any idea of purgatory can quickly dismiss such an account. Still, for those who take purgatory seriously and know of Padre Pio's ability to read souls, his stigmata, and his reputation for holiness, this story speaks volumes to the efficacy of intercession for the souls in purgatory.

St. Faustina described the visit of a deceased religious sister (from her convent) who appeared briefly to her in her cell "all in flames with her face painfully distorted."[376] A short time later, she reappeared requesting additional prayers, and a final time without any flames, her face radiant, and "eyes beaming with joy."[377] The deceased sister encouraged Faustina to pray for the souls in purgatory, which she often did, using indulgenced prayers asking Jesus to free the souls in purgatory.

Faustina also wrote of a visit to purgatory with her guardian angel. She describes fire and a great number of "suffering souls." When asked what caused their greatest torment, Faustina wrote in her Diary (*Divine Mercy in My Soul*) that together they responded: "longing for God,"[378] in perfect agreement with the writing of St. Catherine of Genoa.

The *Divine Mercy Chaplet* came into being through the private revelations of St. Faustina during a time when her prayer life enlarged to include the living, especially those near death.[379] As recorded in her Diary, when Jesus dictated his daily intentions for the Novena of the *Divine Mercy Chaplet*, he asked that on the eighth day, the souls in purgatory be remembered:

> *Today bring to Me the souls who are in the prison of Purgatory, and immerse them in the abyss of My mercy. Let the torrents of My Blood cool down their scorching flames. All these souls are greatly loved by Me. They are making retribution to My justice. It is in your power to bring them relief. Draw all the indulgences from the* treasury *of My Church and offer them on their behalf. Oh, if you only knew the torments they suffer, you would continually offer for them the alms of the spirit and pay*

off their debt to My justice (emphasis added).³⁸⁰

St. Faustina lived at a time when purgatory emphasized divine justice; she added a much-needed dose of divine mercy through her recorded visions and reported tutoring by Jesus. St. Faustina records this beautiful prayer for the souls in purgatory:

> *Eternal Father, turn Your merciful gaze upon the souls suffering in Purgatory, who are enfolded in the Most Compassionate Heart of Jesus. I beg You, by the sorrowful Passion of Jesus Your Son, and by all the bitterness with which His most sacred Soul was flooded, manifest Your mercy to the souls who are under Your just scrutiny. Look upon them in no other way than through the Wounds of Jesus, Your dearly beloved Son; for we firmly believe that there is no limit to Your goodness and compassion.*³⁸¹

It is important to remember that private revelations are just that: private and, even when approved by the Church, are primarily a way that God speaks to a *specific* person in a way that *they* will understand for their spiritual edification. Unlike dogma and doctrine, private revelation is *not* part of the Deposit of Faith.³⁸²

Purgatory may make us squirm while simultaneously fascinating us. Intuitively, we sense that "something [seems] incongruous in the thought that God should inflict the same punishment of those who eternally hate Him and are fixed on evil, and also on those who love Him above all things and are destined to be his companions forever."³⁸³ The *Catechism of the Catholic Church* speaks to a purgatory that quickens our hearts, filling us with confident hope in the generosity of our God—not a purgatory of hell's fire.

Shouldn't *hope*, rather than *fear*, be the overwhelming disposition of our hearts as we contemplate our eternal futures and lift our prayers for our beloved dead to the God of love, forgiveness, mercy, and justice? We must never forget that God knows us better than we know ourselves. Intimately familiar with our failures and sins, he has created a way for us to come to him as a beautified and spotless bride, fully healed from the scabs, scars, and spiritual disfigurement of this life. But we must set our sights higher than purgatory and do our very best to *avoid* purgatory—the topic of Chapter 11.

11 – AVOIDING PURGATORY

The voice of the Holy Spirit is not heard when the message of Thérése of Lisieux ... is thrown to the wind.[384]
                Hans Urs von Balthasar, S.J.

Pope Benedict XVI believed that most people are neither completely permeated by God's love nor already in perfect communion with God and neighbor. Still, neither are they entirely consumed by hatred, suppressing all love within themselves and beyond remedy. However, as he believed, the remediation of purgatory requires an *openness* to God's *love* and his *truth*.[385] That's God's version of the truth, not ours. He wrote:

> *For the great majority of people—we may suppose—there remains in the depths of their being an ultimate interior openness to truth, to love, to God. In the concrete choices of life, however, it is covered over by ever new compromises with evil—much filth covers purity, but the thirst for purity remains and it still constantly re-emerges from all that is base and remains present in the soul. What happens to such individuals when they appear before the Judge? Will all the impurity they have amassed through life suddenly cease to matter? What else might occur?* [386]

After reading the words of Benedict XVI, we might wonder how anyone can avoid purgatory. Someone like me. Someone like you.

Saints such as Teresa of Avila, John of the Cross, and Francis de Sales were of the opinion that few could. Martin Jugie, S.J. (1878-1953), believed that purgatory was an invention of God's infinite mercy but that his preferred plan was for our immediate entry into heaven at death. He wrote that it is "no presumption or lack of humility to desire to conform oneself to the plan of God and avoid

Purgatory ... it is an ambition which honors Christ."[387]

So, if avoiding purgatory should be our goal, how do we do it?

Traditional Channels of Grace

Jugie emphasized the channels of grace instituted by Christ, the sacraments, specifically, Baptism, Reconciliation (Confession), and frequent reception of the Eucharist. He recommended cultivating a spirit of penance, bearing suffering unflinchingly in this life, inculcating the virtue of humility, and praying for the grace of dying well.[388]

The sacraments to help us die well are Anointing of the Sick (Jn 6:54), Reconciliation (Jas 5:14-16), and the Eucharist as Viaticum (Mk 6:13).[389] These three are referred to as the *Last Rites* when collectively administered to those gravely ill. From the earliest days of the apostles, they had anointed the sick among them with oil and prayed over them. For the dying, the *Catechism of the Catholic Church* explains the effects of these sacraments: 1) uniting the person to the passion of Christ, 2) peace, courage, and strengthening for the final journey, and 3) the forgiveness of sin, even if the person cannot confess for medical reasons.[390]

If a person is at the point of death, the attending priest may give an *Apostolic Blessing,* a *plenary indulgence,* also called an *Apostolic Pardon.* As usual, the dying individual must be properly disposed (that is, no attachment to any sin, even venial, and no unconfessed mortal sin). However, if the person is medically unable to confess, receive Holy Communion, or pray for the pope's intentions, those requirements are dispensed.[391] And as with any indulgence, only God knows if it is genuinely granted and exactly how it works.[392]

The priest usually confers an Apostolic Blessing along with the Last Rites. He may use one of two forms when administering. In one form, he prays, "Through the holy mysteries of our redemption, may almighty God release you from all punishments in this life and the life to come. May he open to you the gates of paradise and welcome you to everlasting joy."[393] Sadly, few Catholics know about the Apostolic Blessing and don't know to ask for it should the priest not offer it.

Jugie encourages Masses and prayers to be offered for us while we are *alive*. He challenges us to forgive others, to make amends where possible, to avoid judging others, and to ask for our purgatory on earth.[394] Asking for our purgatory on earth is asking to be perfected in love, which is the point of purgatory.

A half-century before Jugie penned his advice, F.X. Schouppe, S.J. (1823-1904), listed the "exercises and good works which most assist us" to make satisfaction for our sins in this life and to find mercy from God in the afterlife: "devotion to the Blessed Virgin Mary, and fidelity in wearing her [brown]scapular;[395] charity towards the living and the dead; mortification and obedience; a pious reception of the sacraments, especially on the approach of death; confidence in the Divine Mercy; and, finally, the holy acceptance of death in union with the death of Jesus upon the cross."[396]

Since the Middle Ages, Mary (in the devotion to Our Lady of Mt. Carmel) has been associated with relief for the souls in purgatory and the Sabbatine privilege for those who wear the brown scapular and fulfill the rigorous preconditions.[397] Wearing the brown scapular is "an external sign of the filial relationship established between the Blessed Virgin Mary, Mother and Queen of Mount Carmel, and the faithful who *entrust themselves totally* to her protection, who have recourse to her maternal intercession, who are mindful of the primacy of the spiritual life and the need for prayer (emphasis added)."[398] The Church teaches that Mary is our spiritual mother, modeling humility and leading us to Christ. St. Louis de Montfort (1673-1716) and Pope St. John Paul II encouraged total entrustment to Mary, as does Fr. Michael Gaitley, MIC, through the *Consecration of Jesus through the Immaculate Heart of Mary*.[399]

The "Little Way"

To avoid purgatory altogether, Jugie recommended the spiritual childhood or the "Little Way" of St. Thérèse of Lisieux (1873-1897). St. Therese was proclaimed a Doctor of the Church in 1997, the youngest of four women to share that honor. Jugie characterized her life as a "sublime example" of little acts "of humble and peaceful repentance, of childlike confidence and filial love," which were "more powerful for the cleansing of a fault than a mountain of bitter contrition and crushing impatience with self, which merely hinders the soul in its flight to Christ."[400]

I first discovered St. Thérèse's theology and spirituality through

Fr. Michael Gaitley's book *33 Days to Merciful Love*. Thérèse's goal was to become a great saint. She believed avoiding purgatory was possible because she trusted that Jesus would not give her the desire to go directly to heaven at her death unless he also provided the means. In her "Little Way" of complete trust in Jesus, we see the embodiment of Matthew 18:3: *Truly I tell you, unless you change and become like children, you will never enter the kingdom of heaven.*

Thérèse knew her frailties, weaknesses, and "nothingness" (her terminology) well. She trusted God's mercy to bypass the punishment his justice demanded by her sins, and at her death, to take her straight to heaven. She died at age 24 from pulmonary tuberculosis that had spread to her intestines, a most excruciating condition. Her spirituality was remarkable for one so young, but also because the Satisfaction Model of purgatory and the remnants of Jansenism (which presented a harsh view of God) prevailed in France during her lifetime.

Her autobiography, *The Story of a Soul*, was written in obedience to her superiors. Many publishers augment the autobiographical content with appendices containing recollections of Thérèse by those who lived with her; a bevy of letters she composed to friends, family, and other religious; and prayers she wrote. This assemblage documents her spirituality and testifies to her astounding wisdom, love, and absolute childlike trust in Jesus.

Her writings embody 2 Corinthians 12:9-10, where Christ assures Paul, *My grace is sufficient for you, for power is made perfect in weakness*. Paul then responds, *So, I will boast all the more gladly of my weaknesses, so that the power of Christ may dwell in me. Therefore, I am content with weaknesses, insults, hardships, persecutions, and calamities for the sake of Christ; for whenever I am weak, then I am strong.*

Thérèse did not arrive at her "Little Way" overnight. It was the work of her lifetime, consisting of many trials, including the early loss of her mother, emotional fragility, and scrupulosity.[401] In her autobiography, Thérèse wrote, "I had to pass through many trials before reaching the haven of peace, before tasting the delicious fruits of *perfect love* and of *complete abandonment to God's Will* (emphasis added.)"[402]

It was in perfect abandonment to God's will that Thérèse's desires of "self" became lost in her Divine Spouse, and the flower of love bloomed profusely. She wrote, "The spirit of self-abandonment alone is my guide. I have no other compass, and know not how to ask anything with eagerness, save the perfect accomplishment of God's designs upon my soul."[403]

In her work with novices, Thérèse encouraged the young women to be confident that they could avoid purgatory. One young novice lamented failing even in the smallest things and, thus, despaired of any hope of going straight to heaven. Thérèse, who knew well the struggles of her novice, replied: "Yes! God is so good. He will know how He can come and get you. But despite this, try to be faithful, so that He does not wait in vain for your love."[404]

Thérèse's thoughts on avoiding purgatory were not always well received by the sisters in her cloistered Carmelite convent. Sr. M. Fébronie, a sixty-something sub-prioress, reproached Thérèse for her presumptuous confidence. Thérèse's calm but bold response was, "You desire God's justice, so you will have God's justice. The soul receives precisely what it expects from God."[405]

According to Thérèse, one cannot go to purgatory if one loves. To understand what this kind of *love* entails for her, we must study her life, the witness of others, her Act of Oblation,[406] and the intense spiritual and physical suffering God exacted from Thérèse at the end of her life. Within this context, Thérèse transforms what may sound to some like presumption into a hymn of glory, gratitude, and the complete conformance of her will to God's.

Thérèse didn't deny God's justice. Indeed, she felt justice was what she deserved. According to Fr. Michael Gaitley, MIC, her spirituality was based on *trying and never giving up*, with faithfulness to God's commandments, resolving to avoid sin, and possessing sincere sorrow when she did sin.[407] With this firm amendment, she had confidence in God's "Merciful Love." Thérèse's God was not the Santa-Claus god, invented by popular culture, who is too gentle to be offended by sin and whose justice is blinded by love.

On June 9, 1895, with the permission of her superior, Thérèse offered herself as a "Victim of Holocaust to God's Merciful Love."[408] Her exact prayer, an Act of Oblation, was found in her copy of the Gospels after her death. A small extract follows:

In order to live in one single act of perfect Love, I offer myself as a victim of holocaust to Thy Merciful Love, imploring Thee to consume me incessantly, allowing the floods of infinite tenderness shut up within Thee to overflow into my soul, and that thus I may become a martyr of Thy Love, O my God! May this martyrdom, after having prepared me to appear in Thy presence, free me from this life at last and may my soul take its flight—without delay—into the eternal embrace of Thy Merciful Love.[409]

After making her Act of Oblation, she wrote, "[e]very moment this Merciful Love renews me and purifies me, leaving in my soul no trace of sin. I cannot fear Purgatory; I know I do not merit to enter, even, into that place of expiation with the Holy Souls, but I also know that the *fire of Love* is more sanctifying than the *fire of Purgatory* (emphasis added)."[410]

This "fire of Love" is reminiscent of St. John of the Cross and the writings of Benedict XVI in *Spe Salvi*. St. John of the Cross, OCD (1542-1591), was a contemporary and friend of St. Teresa of Avila. John compared purgatory to the *dark night of the soul*. For John, souls in purgatory are purified by fire, but for a person still living on earth, the soul is purified by love.[411] He emphasized that the purification on earth bequeaths infinite merits to the soul.[412] Thérèse's motto, "Love is repaid by love alone," was borrowed from St. John of the Cross."[413]

From April 3, 1896 (Good Friday), until her death on September 30, 1897, Thérèse went through her own dark night of the soul. Amidst her physical agony, she experienced the torment of doubting the truths of her faith, including the existence of heaven, and feeling abandoned by the hiddenness of her Spouse when she needed him most. Yet, persevering, she found God's strength in her final weakness. She wrote that "to dedicate oneself as a Victim of Love is not to be dedicated to sweetness and consolations; it is to offer oneself to all that is painful and bitter, because Love lives only by sacrifice ... and the more we would surrender ourselves to Love, the more we must surrender ourselves to suffering."[414]

God allowed Thérèse to suffer terribly at the end; this was testified by those present. Reading the eyewitness accounts left this reader immensely moved.[415] It is not difficult to believe that the Lord took Thérèse's Act of Oblation quite seriously and that, upon her death, purgatory held no additional work for her. The time between her death and canonization was only 28 years.

12 – CONCLUSION

For many, the doctrine of Purgatory has lost credibility. The language of 'punishment due to sin' and making satisfaction for sin, and of souls suffering for a period of time, sounds to many quite anachronistic. ... In a word, the question must be asked: Is the doctrine of Purgatory worth retrieving or can it ... be quietly forgotten about? [416]
Dermot Lane

As Christians, we believe that we were created by and for God, to be in eternal communion with him, for he is himself a communion of love: Father, Son, and Holy Spirit. God is the Absolute Good toward which all creation is directed and will ultimately return. Our wounded human nature fights against the Absolute Good for which we were created, and like St. Paul, we may not want to sin, but lesser goods, presented by the intellect, sway our weakened will to "bite the apple of temptation." (cf. Rom 7:15-21) Thus, daily, we confront our weakness and propensity to sin.

Without grace, human nature resists sacrifice and suffering *in this life*, even if a greater good is to be had. Obvious examples impacting our body include avoiding exercise and eating unhealthy food even when we desire to look and feel our best. Examples affecting our soul include unforgiveness when others have wronged us, refusing to apologize and make amends when we have wronged others, hiding our failures from others, and justifying our wrongdoings to ourselves. These latter examples testify to 1) our imperfect love for God and others, 2) unhealthy self-love, and 3) that protecting our pride is serious business. Such is the inner tension between behavior and intention.

Making progress in love and humility involves a kind of suffering—a dying to self that ironically births healthy self-love—

leading to Christ-like character transformation. We have limited days on earth to embark and attempt to complete this transformative journey, albeit one baby step at a time. It is seductive to reject the idea of transformation *after this life* to finish the process, should that process involve pain, especially given the pain involved with making small steps toward character re-formation *in this life*.

All Christians agree that our salvation is made possible through Christ's atoning work on the cross. But how Christians understand the mystery of being made holy enough for heaven is encumbered with different theologies of justification, righteousness, sanctification, and ultimately, acceptance or rejection of purgatory.

Aquinas believed (and the Church teaches) that the will's assent of faith *justifies* us. But those God takes to himself in his justice and mercy are made *righteous* and *sanctified* through our *cooperation* with God's grace. This transformation occurs in such a way that reforms both our will and intellect, ultimately eradicating all vestiges of sin and enabling our communion with God in the beatific vision. This process takes time, "extending through this life and continuing in the next."[417] In other words, if sanctification (or sainthood) doesn't happen in this life and we die as God's friends (in a state of grace), we can be sure that God will not abandon us—he will finish the process in purgatory.

This postmortem transformative process to bridge the gap between our imperfect love and our deficiency of holiness eventually became known as purgatory and was declared a dogma of the Catholic Church at the Council of Florence and reaffirmed at the Council of Trent. Most Protestant theology rejects the need for purgatory; sadly, many Catholics agree.

To dismiss purgatory altogether is to misunderstand the nature of sin and human psychology, to close one's mind to the Holy Spirit guiding the Church in her teachings, and to cast aside the many insights from philosophers, theologians, and saints from the earliest times to the present. That is not to deny that in the past, there have been "gross exaggerations in popular preaching and teaching about Purgatory and that more was said about the pain of purgatory than about the love and mercy of God."[418] Modern theologians and the *Catechism of the Catholic Church* present a purgatory seeped in Christology, not a place, but a state of transformation. This is not a "new" purgatory but a deeper understanding of it.

The writings of some Protestant philosophers of religion advance

Christian anthropological arguments for purgatory. Unable to draw upon a claim of Catholic dogma, these philosophers make a compelling case for a Sanctification Model, citing the soul's preservation of self-identity and God's respect for our free will in the afterlife. Examples include C.S. Lewis, David Brown, Jerry Walls, Justin Barnard, and others. The Sanctification Model of purgatory that they argue for distances itself from any hint of temporal punishment for sin—or the Satisfaction Model. Perhaps this need to reject Catholic purgatory (an identification or unification of satisfaction *and* sanctification) is partly due to an incomplete understanding of temporal punishment and Catholic purgatory. The need for differentiation is undoubtedly further "stoked" by the historical baggage that purgatory and indulgences carry in Protestant circles.

Around the time of Vatican II, Catholic theologians reimagined purgatory through a more pastoral slant as "a confirmation of God's initial creating love for the world, and conveying His continued care for its inhabitants—especially [for] those in need of further personal development and/or healing."[419] In that light, purgatory becomes more than simply a required dogma of faith but a compassionate and constructive way to respond to the lay faithful's "personal hopes, fears, and circumstances as they transition to the afterlife in their ongoing journey towards God."[420]

As a cradle Catholic who walked away from the Christian faith, then walked back (thanks be to God!)—first as an Evangelical and then, eventually, all the way back to her Catholic roots—I have found the concept of *redemptive suffering* one of the many priceless treasures of my Catholic faith. After two years of research, I now add *purgatory* as another, and I believe they are related. To understand the Unified Model of purgatory, proclaimed as dogma, in which the Sanctification and Satisfaction Model are the same (as Judisch argues), we must accept the mystery of redemptive suffering. We accept it in Christ's work on the Cross, but do we accept it as the transformative work of suffering in ourselves?

In his encyclical *Evangelium Vitae* (*The Gospel of Life*), Pope John Paul II wrote:

Living to the Lord also means recognizing that suffering, while still an evil and a trial in itself, can always become a source of good. It becomes such if it is experienced for love and with love through sharing, by God's gracious gift and one's own personal and free choice, in the suffering of

Christ Crucified. In this way, the person who lives his suffering in the Lord grows more fully conformed to him (cf. Phil 3:10; 1 Pet 2:21) and more closely associated with his redemptive work on behalf of the Church and humanity.[421]

God the Father could have chosen any way to redeem us after the Fall. (cf. Gen 3) However, he asked his only begotten Son to take on human flesh, suffer, and die an ignominious and excruciating death. The Father loves the Son perfectly, yet this was His plan for our salvation, to which the Son agreed. This alone tells us that suffering and love are united in a profound divine mystery. The mystery of suffering shrouds "purgatory" on earth and in the afterlife.

St. Faustina Kowalska wrote that suffering "is a great grace; through suffering the soul becomes like the Savior; in suffering love becomes crystallized; the greater the suffering, the purer the love."[422] The life and wise words of St. Thérèse of Lisieux are a window into redemptive suffering. Very near the end of her life, while enduring horrific pain, Thérèse remarked to her mother superior, "Do not be troubled ... if I suffer much and show no sign of happiness at the end. Did not Our Lord Himself die 'a Victim of Love,' and see how great was His Agony!"[423]

It is certainly possible to avoid purgatory, but it will require that we abandon ourselves entirely to God's will and perfect our love on this side of the grave. The *work* of the "Little Way" consists *not* in doing extraordinary things but in small things—mired in the mundane and monotonous, camouflaged in the daily surrender to the ordinary, and seeped in trust and joyful acceptance of all that God sends our way even when that involves physical, spiritual, and emotional suffering.

We don't have the power to do this *work* on our own, but only through our cooperation with God's grace and the *confidence* that he will supply what we need in our "littleness" and "nothingness." We must trust the workings of his love. Thérèse understood that our hands are empty, save God's work through and in us.

The theology of Thérèse is the Catholic answer to the Protestant Reformation.[424] Only in God's grace are we saved, and our merits are only those that he accomplishes in us. But that does not mean that faith alone saves, for the fruits of faith are abandonment to God's will, trust and hope in God to save me from myself, and an evident outpouring of love in what I think, say, and do. Such is the paradox of the "Little Way." Only those who do the will of the Father and become as little children will enter the kingdom of heaven. (cf. Mt 7:21, Mt 18:3)

As C. S. Lewis observed, God's work will not stop for those who love him until his work is complete in us. We will be perfected in holiness through him, with him, and in him. Anything preventing the *union* with our Beloved—the temporal remains of our sin—will be removed—by whatever it takes, for God loves us too much to keep anything in the way of our union with him.

To conform our wills and hearts *perfectly* to the Father's is our work on earth, and if achieved here, we will have perfect trust, total abandonment to God, and his effusive love. Purgatory's "work" shall have been completed.

What should we expect? We can look to Christ—fully human yet fully divine. Scripture describes the burden imposed on Christ's human nature in his agony in the Garden of Gethsemane:

Father, if you are willing, remove this cup from me; yet, not my will but yours be done." Then an angel from heaven appeared to him and gave him strength. In his anguish he prayed more earnestly, and his sweat became like great drops of blood falling down on the ground. (Lk 22: 42-45)

We should expect our own Gethsemane as we labor to conform our wills and intellect to Christ's. If we consider Thérèse of Lisieux's "Little Way" as a road to sanctity and sainthood—to be consumed by Divine Love—we can glimpse the "cost." She wrote in 1885:

This aspiration [of sainthood] may very well appear rash, seeing how imperfect I was, and am, even now, after so many years of religious life; yet I still feel the same daring confidence that one day I shall become a great Saint. I am not trusting in my own merits, for I have none; but I trust in Him Who is Virtue and Holiness itself. It is He alone Who, pleased with my feeble efforts, will raise me to Himself, and, by clothing me with His merits, make me a Saint. At that time, I did not realise that to become one [a saint] *it is necessary to suffer a great deal; but God soon disclosed this secret to me by means of the trials I have related.*[425]

Thérèse identified herself as a "Victim of Love"[426] at the cost of climbing the steep hill to self-surrender. For Thérèse, God's love was synonymous with his mercy, yet she declared, "Our Lord is Justice itself."[427]

The God of Thérèse has not been disrobed of justice and

crowned only with mercy, too kindly to permit any suffering for a greater good and too accepting to call some sins mortally wounding. God created us to image him; God does not image us. We are the part; God is the infinite whole. To anthropomorphize and "tame" God misses the unity of all he is, the inseparability of his justice, mercy, and the beauty of his gift of purgatory. In our attempt to "render" a God that we do not fear, we dissect his justice from his mercy and create two dueling models of purgatory: sanctification and satisfaction.

Von Balthazar wrote that the apparent antithesis between God's justice and mercy is removed "existentially" in supernatural hope. And that hope, dear reader, is purgatory:

One who looks only at the justice of God is as little able to hope as is one who sees only the mercy of God. Both fall prey to hopelessness—one to the hopelessness of despair, the other to the hopelessness of presumption. Only hope is able to comprehend the reality of God that surpasses all antithesis, to know that his mercy is identical with his justice and his justice with his mercy.[428]

Precisely how suffrages help facilitate the "work of purgatory" is a mystery. Might our suffrages for the dead (expressed as Masses for the dead, self-mortifications, prayers, and indulgences) encourage and reassure souls as they embark on the postmortem journey to align their wills, intellects, and love to image Christ? Might our prayerful remembrances make it easier for souls to assimilate the unlearned lessons of charity obscured by past sins in this life?

The Church, in her wisdom and guided by the Holy Spirit, has encouraged us to follow the natural prompting of our hearts by offering prayers for our beloved dead. As we pray for the living, so we pray for the dead. Indulgences, regardless of past abuses, are a formalized way of the same. If God is love (and he is), how can our ties to our beloved family and friends be broken if their souls are now in God's hands?

During a general audience in 1999, Pope John Paul II said that "Jesus, as the great intercessor who atones for us, will fully reveal himself at the end of our life when he will express himself with the offer of mercy, but also with the inevitable judgment for those who refuse the Father's love and forgiveness."[429] Reading those words, I ponder who would refuse such an offer. Perhaps accepting the painful truth and owning the wake of destruction for past sins is rejected due to pride. As the *Catechism* states, "Hatred of God comes from pride."[430]

In our faith and hope, death becomes our door to eternity. Binding our fear of death and its commensurate pain to our faith and hope in Christ is our last test and is laden with transformative power. Our death becomes our final act of redemptive suffering for us or offered for others.

Purgatory "Found"

Eschatology is the theological study of the "Last Things." For the *individual*, this includes death and the afterlife: purgatory, heaven, and hell. But a broader category consists of all of *humanity* and *creation*—the climax of all history or what theologians term the *eschaton*. Since Vatican II, the central theme of Catholic eschatology has emphasized this more comprehensive interpretation, where the victory of grace over sin and death is directed towards a new creation proclaiming "the blessedness of union with God, one divine destiny revealed in the risen Christ who is the *eschaton in person*."[431] And that is where purgatory has been, not hidden but expanded.

We have food for our journey to these "Last Things." Jesus left us with the great gift of his Body and Blood to strengthen us in our earthly task to remake ourselves in his image. Theologian Henry Novella wrote that it is the Eucharist, which "keeps alive Christian hope in the final coming of God's Reign in the new creation, and unites the past and the future in the present. ... Until that day comes, we must strain forward in *imitation of Christ* so as to give hopeful witness in the world to the truth, goodness, and beauty of what has taken place in Christ's life, death, and resurrection from the dead in the power of the Spirit (emphasis added)."[432]

We shall achieve the ultimate meaning, purpose, and joy of our lives by imitating Christ's love, sacrifice, and humility. (cf. Phil 2:5-8) My prayer for all of us is that we remain open to *Absolute Truth*, eager to remake ourselves into the image of Christ.

Through faith, we are assured of all we hope for in the life to come and the conviction of things unseen. (cf. Heb 1:11) Jesus is the wellspring of our trust that God will accompany those who love him all the way to perfect sanctity either in this life or the next. And so, we discover purgatory is not a frightening, fiery furnace but a Divine Beauty Parlor where Perfect Love readies us for union with our

Beloved Spouse and to celebrate the marriage feast of the Lamb.

Acknowledgments

This book has been long in preparation. First and foremost, I must recognize my husband's contribution throughout the research stage, the writing phase, and the tedious revision process. He has endured many dinner conversations about purgatory with thoughtful participation and convincing interest. His seemingly infinite patience with my laser focus (bordering on obsession) with this project did not go unnoticed. As an ex-Protestant pastor, holding an MDiv from Fuller Seminary and in full communion with the Catholic Church since 2013, his meticulous and pointed critiques made this book much better than it would have been otherwise. Thank you, Neal, a gazillion times over.

A big thank you goes out to my editor, Patrice Fagnant-MacArthur. Your master's degree in applied theology must have come in handy with editing this book! With gratitude, I acknowledge my proofreader, Ellen Gable Hrkach. Hannah Linder modified my draft cover and perfected it! She has the Midas touch. Thanks to my daughter Bernadette for connecting *Les Misérables* to the concept for the cover of this book, pointing out the symbolism of working out one's "purgatory" on earth, and ultimately suggesting the epigraph.

Thanks to Rev. Matthew O'Leary for his inspirational lectures on Church history, answering my occasional, random questions, and deciphering the Latin text in Figure 1. A nod goes out to Rev. Rob Evenson. The ecumenical "flavor" of your sermons at daily Mass was refreshing and appreciated.

Although not a person, per se, I wish to gratefully acknowledge the rich resources available through my local library via their interlibrary loan program, effectively opening university libraries nationwide to me. The online access to peer-reviewed journals through my local library was similarly invaluable, keeping the price tag of my research manageable. This project would have been impossible without online book depositories, such as the *Wayback Machine Project* of the *Internet Archive* and the *Gutenberg Project*, where I accessed many (old) books or those no longer in print. My research would have been impossible without access to these resources; I do not take them for granted.

Lastly and most importantly, it is only through the grace and redemption of God, through his Son Jesus Christ, that I have eyes to see, ears to hear, and a heart that rests in him amidst the cacophony of this life.

> *In a spirit of thankfulness let me recall the mercies you lavished on me,*
> *O my God; to you let me confess them.*
> *May I be flooded with love for you until my very bones cry out,*
> *"Who is like you, O Lord?"* [433]
>
> St. Augustine of Hippo

About the Author

Meggie K. Daly is a wife, mother, grandmother, practicing Roman Catholic, and independent scholar. During her undergraduate studies at Seattle University, the Jesuits and Dr. Rosaleen Trainor, CSJ, nurtured her love of philosophy, which appealed to her questioning, detail-oriented mind. After earning an advanced degree in mathematics, she worked as a math instructor, research scientist, and applied mathematician in science and technology.

Born into the Catholic faith, she embarked on a unique spiritual journey, departing from her Christian beliefs for approximately ten years. After a profound conversion experience, she found her spiritual home in an Evangelical Church. In 2012, she made a momentous return to her Catholic roots.

Now retired, she writes faith-filled nonfiction. She and her husband, a former Protestant pastor, live in the Pacific Northwest near their newest brood of grandchildren.

Notes

[1] Victor Hugo, trans Lee Fahnestock (et al.), *Les Misérables*, Kindle (New York: Signet Classics—Penguin Group, 2013), 104.

Preface

[2] Ignatius of Antioch, eds. Alexander Roberts and James Donaldson, "The Epistle of Ignatius to the Smyrnaeans," *The Apostolic Fathers: The Ante-Nicene Fathers, Vol. 1* (New York: C. Scribner's Sons: 1913), 89.
[3] Fr. Lorig died in 2019. For additional information, see his autobiography: Fr. Doug Lorig, *Faith's Journey: A Story of Discipleship* (Paradise Valley, AZ: Theosis Press, 2017).
[4] This phrase is borrowed from the subtitle of Jerry L. Walls, *Purgatory: The Logic of Total Transformation* (New York: Oxford University Press, 2012). Early in my research, Walls's book was my "Rosetta Stone" as I labored to integrate my late-1950s-to-early-1960s understanding of purgatory with the gentler words of the *Catechism of the Church* (2000) after returning to the Catholic Church in 2012.

Chapter 1

[5] Jerry L. Walls, "Purgatory for Everyone," *First Things: A Monthly Journal of Religion & Public Life*. Apr 2002, (122), 26.
[6] Karl Rahner, trans. by Karl-H. Kruger, *Theological Investigations: Man in the Church, Vol. 2* (Baltimore, MD: Helicon Press, 1963), 175.
[7] Roy Rivenburg, "Purgatory: After years of neglect, some Protestants now believe it exists; many Catholics don't. For others, it's not a place—it's a state of mind." *Los Angeles Times*, Oct. 20, 1995, LAtimes.com/archives/la-xpm-1995-10-20-ls-59038-story.html.
[8] "U.S. Protestants Are Not Defined by Reformation-Era Controversies 500 Years Later," *Pew Research Center*, Aug 31, 2017, pewresearch.org/religion/2017/08/31/u-s-protestants-are-not-defined-by-reformation-era-controversies-500-years-later.
[9] Lutheran-Catholic Dialogue (Centered Around Human Death and the Promise of Eternal Life), *Hope of Eternal Life* (Ecumenical & Interreligious Affairs of United States Catholic Conference of Bishops, 2010), 213,

usccb.org/committees/ecumenical-interreligious-affairs/hope-eternal-life.
[10] Lutheran-Catholic Dialogue, *Hope of Eternal Life*, 156.
[11] John E. Thiel, "Time, Judgment, and Competitive Spirituality: A Reading of the Development of the Doctrine of Purgatory," *Theological Studies*, Vol. 69, Iss. 4 (2008): 780.
[12] Fr. F. X. Schouppe, S.J., *Purgatory: Explained by the Lives and Legends of the Saints* (Charlotte, North Carolina: Tan Books, 1986), 163. Originally published in London by Publisher Burns, Oats & Washbourne, 1920.
[13] Thomas Aquinas, trans. Fathers of the English Dominican Province, *Summa Theologica (All Complete & Unabridged 3 Parts, Supplement & Appendix*, Kindle (e-artnow, 2013), 7363 (Appendix I q1 a1, *sed contra*).
[14] Henry Novello, "Eschatology Since Vatican II: Saved in Hope," *The Australasian Catholic Record*, Vol. 90, No. 4 (2013): 415.
[15] For additional detail, see Dermot A. Lane, *Keeping Hope Alive: Stirring in Christian Theology* (Mahwah, NJ: Paulist Press, 1996), 1-13 and 132-148.
[16] Thiel, "Time, Judgment, and Competitive Spirituality," 741-742.
[17] John Paul II, *Evangelium Gaudium*, Apostolic Exhortation: The Joy of the Gospel, (Nov. 24, 2013), 64, vatican.va/content/francesco/en/apost_exhortations/documents/papa-francesco_esortazione-ap_20131124_evangelii-gaudium.html#Some_cultural_challenges.
[18] In *Purgatory: The Logic of Total Transformation* by Jerry L. Walls, pages 35-57 provide an excellent review of historical Protestant views on purgatory.
[19] Brian Cross, "Traditions as Paradigms: A MacIntyrean Approach to the Catholic Question," *Faith and Reason: Philosophers Explain Their Turn to Catholicism*, eds. Brian Besong and Jonathan Fuqua, (San Francisco: Ignatius Press, 2019), 260-261.
[20] The converse is false: indulgences are theologically (and philosophically) dependent on the existence of purgatory.

Chapter 2

[21] John Paul II, *Fides Et Ratio*, Encyclical Letter: Faith and Reason, (Sep. 14, 1998), first sentence, vatican.va/content/john-paul-ii/en/encyclicals/documents/hf_jp-ii_enc_14091998_fides-et-ratio.html.
[22] Brian R. Cross, "Traditions as Paradigms," *Faith and Reason*, 249.
[23] Aristotle, trans. Hugh Tredennick, *Aristotle: The Metaphysics, Aristotle, Books I-IX* (London: William Heinemann Ltd, 1933), 163.
[24] Brian Duignan, "Postmodernism," *Encyclopedia Britannica*, (Mar. 21, 2023), britannica.com/topic/postmodernism-philosophy.
[25] My working definition of *metaphysics* is "an idea, doctrine, or posited reality outside of human sense perception. In modern philosophical

terminology, metaphysics refers to the studies of what cannot be reached through objective studies of material reality." This is excerpted from the general glossary provided by PBS's *Faith and Reason* website, pbs.org/faithandreason/gengloss/metaph-body.html.

[26] The branch of philosophy concerned with the theory of knowledge, how we know, and the scope of knowledge is called *epistemology*.

[27] While it is impossible to validate this statistic, the mission statement on the group's website states, "We seek to build a strong community of pro-choice Catholic advocates to promote public policy rooted in true religious liberty, social justice, and respect for conscience."

[28] For a discussion on moral conscience, see: The Catholic Church, *Catechism of the Catholic Church*, 2nd ed. (Washington. D.C.: United States Catholic Conference, 2000), 1776-1802.
(The *Catechism of the Catholic Church* is abbreviated as *CCC* in following endnotes.)

[29] "Christians, religiously unaffiliated differ on whether most things in society can be divided into good, evil," *Pew Research Center*, Dec 21, 2021, pewresearch.org/short-reads/2021/12/21/christians-religiously-unaffiliated-differ-on-whether-most-things-in-society-can-be-divided-into-good-evil/ft_2021-12-21_goodandevil_01/.

[30] "Few Americans Blame God or Say Faith Has Been Shaken Amid Pandemic, Other Tragedies–Views on the Afterlife," *Pew Research Center*, Nov 23, 2021, pewresearch.org/religion/2021/11/23/views-on-the-afterlife/.

[31] Dermot A. Lane, *Keeping Hope Alive*, 43.

[32] The Catholic Church distinguishes between two types of tradition: Sacred Tradition (or big "T" tradition) which doesn't change, and (little "t") tradition which can and has. This difference is further explained in the section "Sacred Tradition" in this chapter.

[33] There was a time when some biblical scholars were of the opinion that the miracles of Christ never happened. I consider this an artifact of the modernist period. For more information, see
reasonablefaith.org/writings/scholarly-writings/historical-jesus/the-problem-of-miracles-a-historical-and-philosophical-perspective.

[34] Orthodox Christians share much in common with the Roman Catholics. The Western Church (the Roman Catholic) and the Eastern Church (the Orthodox) first split in the 1100s, although tensions were evident prior to that. For more information, see "Eastern Orthodox Church," *Wikipedia,* en.wikipedia.org/wiki/Eastern_Orthodox_Church.

[35] For my purposes purgatory and prayers for the dead will be considered separately. If one accepts the existence of purgatory, that does not imply

one believes prayers for the dead are efficacious. Although it is hard to imagine why a Christian would pray for the dead unless one believes that they are not yet in heaven but, also, not in hell.

[36] Note that the Bible itself seems to reject *sola Scriptura*: "So then, brothers and sisters, stand firm and hold fast to the *traditions* that you were taught by us, either by *word of mouth* or by our letter (emphasis added)." (2 Thes 2:15)

[37] Tom Nash, "Who Compiled the Bible and When," *Catholic Answers*, catholic.com/qa/who-compiled-the-bible-and-when.

[38] The biblical books rejected in the Protestant Bible were found in the Septuagint, which was in the Old Testament used by the early Christians, including the apostles, and for the three previous centuries. Ironically these Old Testament books were rejected because Luther felt that they were not sufficiently old. He also concluded that First and Second Maccabees were too new. For a fascinating, in-depth discussion of the Protestant and Catholic biblical canonicity, see Logan Paul Gage, "A Pastor's Kid Finds the Catholic Church," *Faith and Reason: Philosophers Explain Their Turn to Catholicism*, edited by Besong and Fugua (San Francisco: Ignatius Press, 2019),161- 172.

[39] Logan Paul Gage, "A Pastor's Kid Finds the Catholic Church," *Faith and Reason*, 171.

[40] We hear much about synods nowadays, but synods are not ecumenical councils. See Philip Kosloski, "What is the difference between a synod and a council?" Aleteia, Oct 8, 2019, aleteia.org/2019/10/08/what-is-the-difference-between-a-synod-and-a-council.

[41] Here I am using Fr. Gerald L. Orbanek's synthesis of Karl Rahner's words, found in: Fr. Gerald L. Orbanek "The Christology of Paul Tillich: A Critique," *Faith & Reason, The Journal of Christendom College*, Fall 1975, Vol. I, No. 2, 2.

Orbanek is summarizing pages 150-151 from: Karl Rahner, S. J., trans. Cornelius Ernst, OP, *Theological Investigations, God, Christ, Mary, and Grace, Vol. 1* (Baltimore: Helicon Press, 1960).

[42] Rahner, *Theological Investigations, God, Christ, Mary, and Grace, Vol. 1*, 150.

[43] For the 325 AD Nicene Creed due to Hilary of Poitiers, see Henry Denzinger, rev. Karl Rahner, S.J., trans. Roy J. Deferrari, *The Sources of Catholic Dogma (Enchiridion Symbolorum* - 30th edition), Fitzwilliam, NH: Loretto Publications, 2002), 54, which is a republication of Denzinger, *Enchiridion Symbolorum*, 30th edition, (Freiburg: Herder & Co, 1954).

[44] I believe that acceptance of the Trinity is essential to Christianity, not

simply some mainstream "flavor" of Christianity. Others may disagree: "Nontrinitarianism." Wikipedia, Wikimedia Foundation, en.wikipedia.org/wiki/Nontrinitarianism.

[45] Council Fathers, "Second Council of Constantinople – 553 AD," *Papal Encyclicals Online*, papalencyclicals.net/councils/ecum05.htm. Also, see Denzinger, *Sources of Catholic Dogma (Enchiridion Symbolorum)*, 213.

[46] Bryan R. Cross, "Traditions as Paradigms," *Faith and Reason*, 262.

[47] Charlotte Hansen, "Newman, Conscience and Authority," *New Blackfriars*, Vol. 92, No. 1038, (2011): 209-223.

[48] Brian Cutter, "Down the Labyrinthine Ways," *Faith and Reason*, edited by Besong and Fugua (San Francisco: Ignatius Press, 2019), 95.

[49] *CCC*, 88.

[50] W. Scott Cleveland, "A Marriage of Faith and Reason: One Couple's Journey to the Catholic Church, *Faith and Reason: Philosophers Explain Their Turn to Catholicism*, edited by Besong and Fugua (San Francisco: Ignatius Press, 2019), 232-233.

[51] The dogma of papal infallibility was declared in 1870 during the First Vatican Council. Only twice in the history of the Church has papal infallibility been invoked by a pope. The first time was in 1854 when Pope Pius IX declared the dogma of the Immaculate Conception; the second time was in 1950 when Pope Pius XII defined the dogma of the Assumption of Mary. Although both had been believed and accepted as doctrine since the time of early Church. Note that the Church has *never* held that the *opinions* of the pope are infallible.

[52] An interesting discussion on these extremes may be found here: Pope Benedict XVI, *Two Theological Models in Comparison: Bernard and Abelard*, General Audience (Nov 4, 2009), vaticano.va/content/benedict-xvi/en/audiences/2009/documents/hf_ben-xvi_aud_20091104.html.

Chapter 3

[53] Paul Tillich, *The Shaking of The Foundations* (New York: Charles Scribner's Sons, 1953), 154.

[54] The quote "The Church is a hospital for sinners, not a museum for saints" is attributed to Pauline Phillips, who wrote the *Dear Abby* advice column from 1956-2000. Pope Francis made a similar statement describing the Church as a field hospital in an interview with Fr Antonio Spadaro, Sep. 9, 2013, vaticano.va/content/francesco/en/speeches/2013/september/documents/papa-francesco_20130921_intervista-spadaro.html.

[55] This is my restatement of *CCC*, 1472. The full sentence is "A conversion which proceeds from a fervent charity can attain the complete

purification of the sinner in such a way that no punishment would remain." The "punishment" refers to temporal punishment which I explain later in this chapter.

[56] Hilary Brand, "Whatever Happened to Sin? An Examination of the Word and Concept in Contemporary Popular Culture," *Holiness*, Vol. 2, Iss. 3 (2016): 283.

[57] Here I am paraphrasing points made by Bishop Andrew Cozzens, "The Gift of Repentance," *The Catholic Spirit*, Feb. 11, 2021, thecatholicspirit.com/only-jesus/the-gift-of-repentance.

[58] The theology of concupiscence and original sin is also found in Lutheran, Anglican, Methodist, and Reformed faith traditions. However, some Protestant traditions still follow Martin Luther's very pessimistic view of humanity that man has no true free will due to his thorough moral depravity. A corollary to Luther's position is that man can perform no meritorious act.

[59] Disobedience and pride are the most common sins imputed to our first parents in interpreting the Genesis account.

[60] For a comprehensive discussion that covers many faith traditions, see "Original Sin," *Wikipedia*, en.wikipedia.org/wiki/Original_sin.

[61] *CCC*, 402-406. The doctrine of original sin is primarily credited to St. Augustine of Hippo in the 5th century and raised to dogma by the Counsel of Trent in the 16th century.

[62] J. Budziszewski, *What We Can't Not Know: A Guide* (Dallas: Spence Publishing Company, 2003), 15.

[63] Budziszewski, *What We Can't Not Know*, 140.

[64] Budziszewski, *What We Can't Not Know*, 140.

[65] See Archbishop George H. Niederauer, "Fundamental Misconceptions about Catholic Teaching on Human Freedom." *Catholic News Agency*, Jan. 14, 2010, catholicnewsagency.com/column/51086/free-will-conscience-and-moral-choice-what-catholics-believe.

[66] St. Jerome, trans. W. H. Fremantle, G. Lewis, and W. G. Martley, *Nicene and Post-Nicene Fathers of the Christian Church, Second Series*, Vol.VI, (New York: The Christian Literature Company, 1893), "Against Jovinianus - Book II," 411.

[67] St. Jerome, "Against Jovinianus–Book II," 411-412.

[68] St. Augustine, ed. Philip Schaff, *Saint Augustin[e]: Anti Pelagian Writings, From Nicene and Post-Nicene Fathers*, First Series, Vol. V (Buffalo, NY: Christian Literature Publishing Co, 1887), "Of the Spirit and the Letter, Ch 48," 104.

[69] St Augustine, ed. Phillip Schaff, *Nicene and Post-Nicene Fathers of the Christian Church, First Series, Vol. III* (Buffalo, NY: The Christian Literature

Co, 1887), "On the Creed: A Sermon to Catechumens on the Creed," 374-375.

[70] Caesarius of Arles, trans. Sr. Mary Magdelein Mueller, OSF, *The Fathers of the Church: A New Translation, Vol. I* (New York: Fathers of the Church, Inc, 1956). See "Saint Caesarius of Arles: Sermons," on pg. 98, *criminal capitalia* is translated as capital crimes; on page 224, lesser sins are differentiated from capital offenses. Also, Jacques Le Goff, trans. Arthur Goldhammer, *The Birth of Purgatory* (Chicago: University of Chicago Press, 1981), 87 corroborates.

[71] St. Gregory the Great, intro. Edmund G. Gardner, *The Dialogues of St. Gregory The Great* (London: Phillip Lee Warner, 1911), 233.

[72] Gregory the Great, trans. anonymous, ed. Paul A. Böer, Sr., *Morals on the Book of Job*, Kindle (Edmond, OK: Veritatis Splendor Publications, 2012), Vol. III, Bk. XXXI, Sec. XLV, para. 84. (loc 33668/37526)

[73] Aquinas, *Summa Theologica*, 2434 (II-I q88 a4, *sed contra*).

[74] The Council of Trent uses the terminology of venial sin and mortal sin, clarifying the difference between the two and the different requirements to heal the soul from their effects. See Trent's Session XIV, Chapter V, on Confession, Nov. 25, 1551, ewtn.com/catholicism/library/fourteenth-session-of-the-council-of-trent-1480.

[75] *CCC*, 1861.

[76] The Church teaches that *imperfect* contrition (a desire not to sin for reasons other than the love of God) is sufficient to remove even the guilt of mortal sin before God *with* the reception of the Sacrament of Reconciliation. But *perfect* contrition "arises from a love by which God is loved above all else. Perfect contrition remits venial sins; it also obtains forgiveness of mortal sins if it includes the firm resolution to have recourse to sacramental confession as soon as possible." [*CCC*, 1452]

[77] The guilt of sin before God and the consequences of sin (its temporal punishment) were not initially separated in the Church. Only with the completion of the assigned penance for confessed grave sin was the guilt before God thought to be removed. This took several hundred years to sort out in the early Church. This is discussed in this chapter's section, "Historical Development of Temporal Punishment." Also, see Karl Rahner, *Theological Investigations: Man in the Church*, Vol. 2, 195.

[78] For an insightful and cogent explanation of these two schools of Protestant thought, see: Brian Cross, "*Why John Calvin did not Recognize the Distinction Between Mortal and Venial Sin*," Called to Communion: Rome meets the Reformation (Nov. 10, 2011), calledtocommunion.com/2011/11/why-john-calvin-did-not-recognize-the-distinction-between-mortal-and-venial-sin.

[79] *CCC*, 1472.
[80] *CCC*, 1472.
[81] Neal Judisch, "Sanctification, Satisfaction, and the Purpose of Purgatory," *Faith and Philosophy: Journal of the Society of Christian Philosophers*, Vol. 26, Iss. 2, Article 4, (2009): 176.
[82] Romano Guardini, trans. Charlotte E. Forsyth and Grace B. Branham, *The Last Things: Concerning Death, Purification, after Death, Resurrection, Judgment, and Eternity*, Kindle (Providence, Rhode Island: Cluny Media Publications, 2022), 42.
[83] See Hebrews 12:5-6.
[84] Rahner, *Theological Investigations: Man in the Church*, 192.
[85] *CCC*, 1473.
[86] Nicholas A. Jesson, "Paradise Regained: Indulgences in Light of the Joint Declaration on Justification," University of St. Michael's College, Toronto School of Theology, (May 2002), 4, ecumenism.net/archive/jesson_indulgences.pdf.
[87] Jesson, "Paradise Regained," 4.
[88] Rahner, *Theological Investigations: Man in the Church*, 181.
[89] For a detailed explanation of this process, see Jesson, "Paradise Regained: Indulgences in Light of the Joint Declaration on Justification," 2-6.
[90] Rahner, *Theological Investigations: Man in the Church*, 181.
[91] Jesson, "Paradise Regained," 8.
[92] Aquinas writes, "The intensity of contrition may be regarded in two ways. First, on the part of charity, which causes the displeasure, and in this way it may happen that the act of charity is so intense that the contrition resulting therefrom merits not only the *removal of guilt*, but also the *remission of all punishment*. Secondly, on the part of the sensible sorrow, which the will excites in contrition: and since this sorrow is also a kind of punishment, it may be so intense as to suffice for the remission of both *guilt* and *punishment* (emphasis added)." Quoted from *Summa Theologica*, 6296 (Sup III q5 a2, *sed contra*).

Chapter 4

[93] Joseph Ratzinger, *Eschatology: Death and Eternal Life*, 2nd ed. (Washington, D.C., Catholic University Press, 1988), 229.
[94] Lutheran-Catholic Dialogue, *Hope of Eternal Life*, 156.
[95] The debt of temporal punishment need not be separate from purification. In Chapter 5, however, arguments are presented that they are one and the same.
[96] John Calvin, trans. John Allen, *Institutes of the Christian Religion*

(Philadelphia: Presbyterian Board of Publication, 1909), 607.
[97] Justin D Barnard, "Purgatory and the Dilemma of Sanctification," *Faith and Philosophy: Journal of the Society of Christian Philosophers*, Vol. 24: Iss. 3, Article 6 (2007), 314.
[98] "Justification (Theology)," *Wikipedia*, en.wikipedia.org/wiki/Justification_(theology).
[99] *CCC*, 1989.
[100] *CCC*, 1990.
[101] *CCC*, 1993.
[102] Peter Kreeft, "Why?" *Faith and Reason: Philosophers Explain Their Turn to Catholicism* (San Francisco: Ignatius Press, 2019), 135.
[103] Jesson, "Paradise Regained," 27.
[104] Charles Hodge, "Justification Is a Forensic Act," monergism.com/justification-forensic-act.
[105] The Orthodox Church includes The Greek Orthodox Church and all existing churches of the Byzantine Rite that are *separated* from Rome. This does not include Byzantine (or Eastern) Rite Catholics, who are in complete union with Rome. The Orthodox Church rejects papal infallibility, papal supremacy, the Immaculate Conception, and purgatory.
[106] Walls, "Purgatory for Everyone," 29.
[107] The rejection is tied up with indulgences as well, the topic of Chapters 8 and 9.
[108] J. Budziszewski, "A Rake's Progress," *Faith and Reason: Philosophers Explain Their Turn to Catholicism* (San Francisco: Ignatius Press, 2019), 71.
[109] Robert C. Koons, "A Lutheran's Path to Catholicism," *Faith and Reason: Philosophers Explain Their Turn to Catholicism* (San Francisco: Ignatius Press, 2019), 176.
[110] Kreeft, "Why?" *Faith and Reason*, 129.
[111] Lutheran World Federation and the Catholic Church, *Joint Declaration on the Doctrine of Justification*, 1997, 40. The Preamble, in paragraph 1, underlies how Martin Luther's theology of justification ruled over everything else in the Protestant Reformation. The common areas of current agreement between Catholics and Lutherans are explicated in paragraphs 19-39, christianunity.va/content/unitacristiani/en/dialoghi/sezione-occidentale/luterani/dialogo/documenti-di-dialogo/1999-dichiarazione-congiunta-sulla-dottrina-della-giustificazion/en.html.
[112] For a summary of the Lutheran denouncement, see "Augsburg Confession." Encyclopedia Britannica, November 8, 2021, britannica.com/topic/Augsburg-Confession.
[113] Lutheran World Federation and the Catholic Church, *Joint Declaration*

on the Doctrine of Justification, Sec. 5: "The Significance and Scope of the Consensus Reached."
[114] J. Budziszewski, "A Rake's Progress," *Faith and Reason*, 77.

Chapter 5

[115] C. S. Lewis, *Letters to Malcolm: Chiefly on Prayer* (New York: Harcourt, Brace, & World, 1964), 108-109.
[116] The beatific vision "is the ultimate direct self-communication of God to the individual person. A person possessing the beatific vision reaches, as a member of redeemed humanity in the communion of saints, perfect salvation in its entirety, i.e., heaven. The notion of vision stresses the intellectual component of salvation, though it encompasses the whole of human experience of joy, happiness coming from seeing God finally face to face and not imperfectly through faith." The source for this quote is "Beatific Vision," Wikipedia, en.wikipedia.org/wiki/Beatific_vision.
[117] Benedict XVI, *Spe Salvi*, Encyclical Letter: Saved by Hope (Nov. 30, 2007), 44, vaticana.va/content/benedict-xvi/en/encyclicals/documents/hf_ben-xvi_enc_20071130_spe-salvi.html.
[118] Peter Kreeft, "Why?" *Faith and Reason*, 129.
[119] Joseph Pieper, trans Sister Mary Frances McCarthy, SND, *On Hope* (San Francisco: Ignatius Press, 1986), 70-71.
[120] Joseph Pieper, *On Hope*, 47.
[121] Hans Urs von Balthazar, trans. Dr. David Kipp, Rev. Lothar Krauth, *Dare We Hope "That All Men Be Saved"?* (San Francisco: Ignatius Press, 1988), 116. Here Balthazar quotes a sermon of St. Augustine on the Psalms.
[122] Matthew Scott Hendzel, "An Exploration of the Roman Catholic Doctrine of Purgatory in Light of Current Issues in Theodicy": PhD diss., (St. Michael's College, University of Toronto, 2019), 80, tspace.library.utoronto.ca/bitstream/1807/99734/3/Hendzel_Matthew_S_201911_PhD_thesis.pdf.
[123] Benedict XVI, *Spe Salvi*, 47.
[124] This was the model of purgatory adhered to by theologian Francisco Suárez, S.J. (1548-1617). More recently, Martin Jugie, S.J. (1878-1953), seemed to favor this model, too. He argues that indulgences cannot do the work of rehabilitation or purification.
[125] Neal Judisch, "Sanctification, Satisfaction, and the Purpose of Purgatory," 184.
[126] Frederick William Faber, CO, *All for Jesus* (Baltimore: John Murphy & Co, 1855), 378. Fr. Faber does not use the exact words "sanctification" or "satisfaction" for the two views (or models). Rather, he describes one

view as punitive, required by God's justice, and similar to a temporary hell; he describes the other as the purgatory of Catherine of Genoa (in her *Treatise on Purgatory*), marked with hope, joy, cleansing, and purification of the soul as it suffers.

[127] Faber, *All for Jesus*, 379.

[128] Faber, *All for Jesus*, 383.

[129] Aquinas, *Summa Theologica*, Appendix 1:7353-7373 and Appendix 2: 7373-7377.

[130] Walls, *Purgatory: The Logic of Total Transformation*, 73. Walls keeps the Sanctification and Satisfaction Models separate but recognizes both elements in Aquinas's model of purgatory. He does not use the terminology Unified Model; that is mine.

[131] The 1881 *Baltimore Catechism* was published 1885 by J. L. Spalding and issued by the Third Plenary Council of Baltimore.

[132] The question-and-answer format was based on the very short catechism of St. Robert Bellarmine, written in 1598 at the request of Pope Clement VIII. Incidentally, Bellarmine only mentioned purgatory once in his catechism within the context of venial sin. He wrote that it "must be purged in this world or in Purgatory." Cardinal Robert Bellarmine, trans. Mark Moorhead, *A Short Catechism of Cardinal Bellarmine*, Kindle (Morehead, 2021) 28. His catechism was originally published in Latin in the year 1614.

[133] For a detailed, but reasonably concise, history of the Baltimore Catechism, see Biff Rocha, *De Concilio's Catechism, Catechists, and the History of the Baltimore Catechism*, PhD diss. (University of Dayton, 2014), pp. 38-42, 254-256, 38-42,

etd.ohiolink.edu/acprod/odb_etd/ws/send_file/send?accession=dayton1386154475.

[134] Third Plenary Council of Baltimore, Rev Thomas. L. Kinkead, *Catechism of the Christian Doctrine* (New York: Benziger Brothers, 1921), sometimes called the *Kinkead Edition*.

[135] *Catechism of the Christian Doctrine, Kinkead Edition*, 307-308. The selected Q&As are from Catechism No. 3, Lesson 37, question numbers are retained as shown. Question 1381 is also found in Catechism No. 2 as question 141; no mention of purgatory is found in Catechism No. 1.

[136] Third Plenary Council of Baltimore, with Rev Francis J. Connell, CSSR., STD., and Rev. David Sharrock, CSSR, *The New Confraternity Edition Revised Baltimore Catechism No. 3* (New York: Benziger Brothers, 1949), Lesson 14, para. 1, "Important Truths about the Resurrection and Life Everlasting"), 201. This edition is often referred to as the *Fr. Connell's Catechism*.

[137] John Paul II, *Fidei Depositum,* Apostolic Constitution: Publication of the Catechism of the Catholic Church prepared following the Second Vatican Ecumenical Council (Oct. 11, 1992), III, vatican.va/content/john-paul-ii/en/apost_constitutions/documents/hf_jp-ii_apc_19921011_fidei-depositum.html.

[138] John Paul II, *Laetamur Magnopere*, Apostolic Letter: The Latin Typical Edition of the *Catechism of the Catholic Church* is approved and promulgated (Aug. 15, 1997), vatican.va/content/john-paul-ii/en/apost_letters/1997/documents/hf_jp-ii_apl_15081997_laetamur.html.

[139] *CCC,* 1030-1032.

[140] 2 Mc 12:46, 1 Cor 41, and Job 1:5.

[141] *CCC,* 1472-1473.

[142] Indulgences, while not a required Catholic practice, were dogmatically confirmed by the Church at the Council of Trent in 1563.

[143] Walls, *Purgatory: The Logic of Total Transformation*, 92. Wall's statement is largely drawn from his reading of the *Catechism of the Catholic Church* and from the theological writings of Pope Benedict XVI, when writing as Joseph Ratzinger.

[144] John Paul II, *Fidei Depositum*, part III.

[145] A *lapsable* person is one who still has some attachments to sin and, thus, remains capable of sin.

[146] Neal Judisch, "Sanctification, Satisfaction, and the Purpose of Purgatory," 178.

[147] Lutheran-Catholic Dialogue, *The Hope of Eternal Life*, 208.

Chapter 6

[148] Karl Rahner, trans. Edward Quinn, *Theological Investigations: Faith and Ministry, Vol. 19* (New York: Crossroad Publishing Company, 1983), 183. In Chapter 14, Rahner constructs an imaginary dialog between two theologians concerning purgatory. The cited quote is a comment where one theologian asks the other theologian what exactly the Catholic Church teaches about purgatory.

[149] Ratzinger, *Eschatology: Death and Eternal Life*, 230. The *Communion of Saints* is the union of all the redeemed, living and dead, united through the Body of Christ. This topic is covered in Chapter 8.

[150] Martin Jugie, *The Truth about Purgatory: And the Means to Avoid It*, Kindle (Manchester, NH: Sophia Institute, 2022), 6. Originally published in 1950 by Newman Press Westminster, Maryland.

[151] Guardini, *The Last Things*, 44.

[152] Eleonore Stump, *Walking in Darkness: Narrative and the Problem of Suffering*, Kindle (Oxford, UK: Oxford University Press, 2012), 91. To support this assertion, she cites the following passages in the *Summa Theologica*: for the willing the good of the beloved: I-II q26 a4 and I-II q28 a4; for desiring union with the beloved: I-II q26 a2 ad2, I-II q28 a1, I-II q66 a6, I-II q70 a3.
[153] Stump, *Walking in Darkness*, 95
[154] Neil Judisch, "Indulgent Love," *Purgatory: Philosophical Dimensions*, eds. Kristof K.P. Vanhoutte, Benjamin W. McGraw (Cham, Switzerland: Palgrave MacMillian, 2017), 101.
[155] Judisch, "Indulgent Love," *Purgatory: Philosophical Dimensions*, 101.
[156] Guardini, *The Last Things*, 45.
[157] Guardini, *The Last Things*, 41.
[158] Guardini, *The Last Things*, 42.
[159] Guardini, *The Last Things*, 43.
[160] Guardini, *The Last Things*, 44.
[161] Guardini, *The Last Things*, 44.
[162] John E. Thiel, *Icons of Hope: The "Last Things" in Catholic Imagination* (Notre Dame, IN: University of Notre Dame Press, 2013), 52. The *Communion of Saints* refers to the redeemed, whether living or dead, united in the Body of Christ.
[163] Thiel, *Icons of Hope*, 94.
[164] Rahner, *Theological Investigations, Man in the Church*, 197-198.
[165] John Paul II, General Audience, Sep. 29, 1999, 2–3, vatican.va/content/john-paul-ii/en/audiences/1999/documents/hf_jp-ii_aud_29091999.html.
[166] Regis Martin, "Of Purgatory and Homage to the Dead", *The Catholic Thing*, Nov. 2, 2016, thecatholicthing.org/2016/11/02/of-purgatory-and-homage-to-the-dead.
[167] Benedict XVI, *Spe Salvi*, 47.
[168] *CCC*, 365.
[169] Neal Judisch, "Sanctification, Satisfaction, and the Purpose of Purgatory," 170-171. For readers desiring a more complete defense of number three, Judisch provides responses to the most common objections on cited pages.
[170] Scriptural support for sanctification in the twinkling of an eye by some Protestants is claimed by 1 Cor 15:52.
[171] Thiel, *Icons of Hope*, 54.
[172] Lane, *Keeping Hope Alive*, 147.
[173] David Brown, "No Heaven without Purgatory," *Religious Studies*, Vol. 21, No. 4 (Dec. 1985), 447.

[174] Brown, "No Heaven without Purgatory," 453.
[175] C. S. Lewis, *Letters to Malcom: Chiefly on Prayer* (New York: Harcourt, Brace & World, 1964), 110.
[176] Brown, "No Heaven without Purgatory," 453-454.
[177] Brown, "No Heaven without Purgatory," 453-454.
[178] Brown, "No Heaven without Purgatory," 454-455.
[179] Brown, "No Heaven without Purgatory," 456.
[180] Barnard, "Purgatory and the Dilemma of Sanctification," 314.
[181] Barnard, "Purgatory and the Dilemma of Sanctification," 311-330.
[182] Barnard, "Purgatory and the Dilemma of Sanctification," 322.
[183] Barnard, "Purgatory and the Dilemma of Sanctification," 312.
[184] Walls, *Purgatory: The Logic of Total Transformation*, 91.
[185] Walls, *Purgatory for Everyone*, 28.
[186] Walls, *Purgatory: The Logic of Total Transformation*, 57.
[187] Eleonore Stump, "Sanctification, Hardening of the Heart, and Frankfurt's Concept of Free Will," *Journal of Philosophy*, Vol. LXXXV, No. 8, 1988, 395-420. Frankfurt emphasizes the structure of the will in defining the person and distinguishes between first and second-order volitions and desires. First-order desires/volitions are acted upon or realized, whereas second-order desires may or may not be. For example, that St. Paul wishes not to sin (second-order desire) but does (first-order volition) illustrates that his first-order desire is discordant with his second-order. Stump, as a Thomist philosopher, has the intellect directing the will. See page 340 for Stump's explanation of how God preserves man's freedom in sanctification and hardening of the heart (mirror opposites) using her revised Frankfurt account.
[188] Eleonore Stump, "Atonement and Justification," in *Trinity, Incarnation, and Atonement*, eds. Ronald J. Feenstra, Cornelius Plantinga, Jr. (Notre Dame, IN: University of Notre Dame Press, 1989), 186-192.
[189] Stump, "Atonement and Justification," 194.
[190] Stump, "Atonement and Justification," 191.
[191] Lewis, *Letters to Malcolm*, 108.
[192] C. S. Lewis, *Mere Christianity* (San Francisco: Harper Collins, 2001), 202.
[193] Lewis, *Letters to Malcolm*, 109.
[194] Walls, *Purgatory: The Logic of Total Transformation*, 91.
[195] P. T. Forsyth, *This Life and the Next: The Effect of Faith in This Life in Another* (Boston: Pilgrim Press, 1948), 37.
[196] Walls, *Purgatory: The Logic of Total Transformation*, 52-53.
[197] John Hick, *Evil and the God of Love* (New York: Palgrave MacMillan, 2010), 347-349.
[198] Hendzel, "An Exploration of the Roman Catholic Doctrine of

Purgatory in Light of Current Issues in Theodicy," 91.

Chapter 7

[199] Isabel Moreira, *Heaven's Purge: Purgatory in Late Antiquity* (New York: Oxford University Press, 2010), 5.
[200] Walls, *Purgatory: The Logic of Total Transformation*, 32.
[201] Jacques Le Goff, trans. Arthur Goldhammer, *The Birth of Purgatory* (Chicago: University of Chicago Press, 1981).
[202] Thiel, *Icons of Hope*, 71.
[203] Ratzinger, *Eschatology: Death and Eternal Life*, 218-219.
[204] St. Robert Bellarmine, S.J., (1542-1621), a Doctor of the Catholic Church, used the following Scriptures as his proof-texts: 2 Mc 12:42-51; 1 Cor 3:15; Mt 5:25 with Lk 12:58; 1 Cor 15:29; Mt 5:22, Lk 16:9, Lk 23:42, Acts 2:24, and Phil 2:10. Bellarmine's "proofs" were formulated in the Catholic response to the Protestant Reformation. His arguments may be found in: St. Robert Bellarmine, S.J., trans. Ryan Grant, *De Controversiis: On Purgatory* (Post Falls, ID: Mediatrix Press, 2017).

For a modern treatment of scriptural exegesis and "proofs" for purgatory from Scripture, see: John Salza, *The Biblical Basis for Purgatory* (Charlotte, NC: Saint Benedict Press, 2009), 95-143. Also, see Karlo Broussard, *Purgatory is for Real: Good News about the Afterlife for Those Who Aren't Perfect Yet* (Catholic Answers Press: El Cajon, CA, 2020), 53-102.
[205] Brian Cross, *"Traditions as Paradigms,"* 260-261.
[206] Here are a few: Col 1:22, 1 Jn 2, Eph 5:25-27, 1 Jn 3:1-3, Jn 15:1-3, 1 Cor 15:62-53, Rom 5:19, Rom 5:30, Lk 23:43.
[207] This concept is expressed by Guardini, *The Last Things*, 34.
[208] Guardini, *The Last Things*, 99.
[209] St. Cyprian, St. Ambrose, St. Jerome, Pope St. Gregory the Great, Origen, and St. Augustine used this verse to argue for purgatorial-like postmortem state according to Dave Armstrong, "11 Descriptive and Clear Bible Passages About Purgatory," *National Catholic Register*, May 7, 2017.
[210] *CCC*, 1030-1032.
[211] Tertullian, St. Cyprian, Origen, St. Ambrose, and St. Jerome used this to this Scripture to argue for an intermediate state according to Dave Armstrong, "11 Descriptive and Clear Bible Passages About Purgatory," *National Catholic Register*, May 7, 2017.
[212] St. Augustine, Pope St. Gregory the Great, the Venerable Bede and St. Bernard, among others used this Scripture according to Dave Armstrong, "11 Descriptive and Clear Bible Passages About Purgatory," *National Catholic Register*, May 7, 2017.

[213] J. Spencer Northcote, D.D., *Epitaphs of the Catacombs or Christian Inscription in Rome during the First Four Centuries* (Edinburgh & London: Ballantyne, Hanson and Co., 1878), 85-86.

[214] As an aside, whether the souls in purgatory may pray for the living is not something the Church has declared with any definitive doctrine. Thomas Aquinas thought they could not, while others like Robert Bellarmine and Francis de Sales thought they could. Many websites today say they can as a matter of fact. However, this is a matter of opinion not church doctrine.

[215] Northcote, D.D., *Epitaphs of the Catacombs or Christian Inscription in Rome during the First Four Centuries*, 73-74.

[216] ___, *The Acts of St. Paul and Thecla*, 7. Note this is a work of historical "fiction," dated from around the end of the 2nd century. Nevertheless, it does demonstrate what people thought at the time.

[217] ___, trans. W. H. Shewring, *The Passion of SS. Perpetua & Felicity, MM.* (London: Sheed & Ward, 1931), 28-30.

[218] Clement of Alexandra is not Clement of Rome, who was a bishop and martyr.

[219] Joseph Ratzinger, *Eschatology: Death and Eternal Life*, 226.

[220] Clement of Alexandra, trans. William Wilson Fathers, eds. Alexander Roberts, James Donaldson, and A. Cleveland Coxe, *Ante-Nicene Fathers, Vol. 2 Fathers of the Second Century: Hermas, Tatian, Athenagoras, Theophilus, and Clement of Alexandria (Entire)*. (New York: Charles Scribner and Sons, 1913), 505.

[221] Walls, *Purgatory: The Logic of Total Transformation*, 14-15. Cyprian had an important role in developing the theology of indulgences as well, which is elaborated in Chapter 9, "The History of Indulgences."

[222] John E. Thiel, "Time, Judgment, and Competitive Spirituality: A Reading of the Development of the Doctrine of Purgatory," 754-755.

[223] For an in-depth treatment of Augustine's influence, see Le Goff, *The Birth of Purgatory*, 61-78.

[224] Jacques Le Goff, *The Birth of Purgatory*, 67-69.

[225] Saint Augustine, translated by Marcus Dods, *City of God* (New York: Modern Library, 2000), (21.13), 955-956

[226] Saint Augustine, *City of God*, (21.13), 956.

[227] Jacques Le Goff, *The Birth of Purgatory*, 84.

[228] St. Augustine, ed. Phillip Schaff, *Nicene and Post-Nicene Fathers Series I, Vol. 8* (Grand Rapids, MI: Christian Classics Ethereal Library, 1888), 220.

[229] St. Gregory the Great, *The Dialogues of St. Gregory The Great*, xxiv-xxv.

[230] St. Gregory the Great, *The Dialogues of St. Gregory The Great*, 233-234. According to Jacque Le Goff in *The Birth of Purgatory*, the original Latin

would have read "purging fires" or "purifying fires" because he maintains the noun "Purgatory" did not occur at the time of Gregory the Great.

[231] St. Gregory the Great, *The Dialogues of St. Gregory The Great*, 252.

[232] Moreira, *Heaven's Purge*, 147-176.

[233] Moreira, *Heaven's Purge*, 148.

[234] Moreira, *Heaven's Purge*, 149-151.

[235] Moreira, *Heaven's Purge*, 152-156.

[236] Moreira, *Heaven's Purge*, 159.

[237] Moreira, *Heaven's Purge*, 159.

[238] Moreira, *Heaven's Purge*, 156-157.

[239] Karen Palmer, "Augustine and Scholasticism," *Diving into Rhetoric: A Rhetorical View of History, Communication, and Composition* (OER: pressbooks.pub, 2020), pressbooks.pub/divingintorhetoric/chapter/augustine-and-scholasticism/#chapter-28-section-2.

[240] Le Goff, *The Birth of Purgatory*, 364.

[241] For more details, see Le Goff, *The Birth of Purgatory*, Appendix 1: 362-366. For my discussion, it matters little whether the Latin usage is as a noun or adjective. My goal is to understand Purgatory's history from the viewpoint of Scripture, Tradition, and the Magisterium. *The Birth of Purgatory* is truly a historical masterpiece, albeit with a secular worldview and its concomitant biases, which are to be expected from an agnostic historian. However, Le Goff's research is compelling, honest, and passionate. He reveals his heart in his last chapter, "Why Purgatory?" 356-360. He died in 2014. As my husband would say, "He is no longer agnostic." May his soul rest in peace.

[242] Gratian, eds. Emil Friedberg and Emil Ludwig Richter, *Decretum Magistri Gratian* (Graz: Akademische Druck-und Verlagsanstalt (ADEVA), 1955), Vol. 1, Col. 728, para: C XXII. The text is in Latin, I have used *Google Translate* for my English translation.

[243] The theological groundwork for indulgences is shored up during this time.

[244] Le Goff, *The Birth of Purgatory*, 249.

[245] Le Goff, *The Birth of Purgatory*, 255.

[246] Le Goff, *The Birth of Purgatory*, 263.

[247] Aquinas, *Summa Theologica*, 5232 (Sup III q5 a2, *sed contra*).

[248] Aquinas, *Summa Theologica*, 7374 (Appendix II q1, *sed contra*).

[249] This split is blamed on disagreements over papal jurisdiction and filioque clause in Nicene Creed. The Greeks maintained that the Holy Spirit proceeded from the Son alone; not from the Father and Son as the Latin Church taught.

[250] Denzinger, *The Sources of Catholic Dogma*, 456.
[251] Karlo Broussard, *Purgatory is for Real*, 133.
[252] Denzinger, *The Sources of Catholic Dogma*, 464.
[253] Denzinger, *The Sources of Catholic Dogma*, 570.
[254] Denzinger, *The Sources of Catholic Dogma*, 693.
[255] The Protestant Reformation is dealt with in Chapter 9, "The History of Indulgences."
[256] Franz Sales Trenkle, "The Council of Trent." *Christian Classics Ethereal Library*, https://www.ccel.org/s/schaff/encyc/encyc12/htm/ii.ii.htm.
[257] Vatican I (1869-1870) was important but not nearly as critical as the Council of Trent for its sweeping doctrinal impact. Vatican I added *Pastor Aeternus* (papal infallibility) and *Dei Fillias* (the relationship between faith and reason) in response to "the rising influence of rationalism, liberalism, and materialism." See "First Vatican Council," Wikipedia, en.wikipedia.org/wiki/First_Vatican_Council.
[258] "The Council of Trent." *Arts and Humanities Through the Eras*. Encyclopedia.com, encyclopedia.com/humanities/culture-magazines/council-trent.
[259] "General Council of Trent: Sixth Session, Council Fathers – 1547," Chapter XVI, On Justification, Canon XXX, 48, papalencyclicals.net/councils/trent/sixth-session.htm.
[260] "General Council of Trent: Twenty-Fifth Session, Council Fathers- 1563," Decree Concerning Purgatory, 232, papalencyclicals.net/councils/trent/twenty-fifth-session.htm.

Chapter 8

[261] John Paul II, *Incarnationis Mysterium*, Bull of Indiction: The Great Jubilee of the Year 2000, Nov. 29, 1998, 9, vatican.va/jubilee_2000/docs/documents/hf_jp-ii_doc_30111998_bolla-jubilee_en.html.
[262] For an explanation of grants and a list of indulgenced acts, see: The Catholic Church, *Manual of Indulgences: Norms and Grants*, trans. 4th ed. (1999) *Enchiridion Indulgentiarum* (Washington, D.C, USCCB: 2006), pp. 25-102.
[263] *CCC*, 1471-1479.
[264] Logically, belief in some kind of Purgatory need not be linked to belief in the efficacy of prayers for the dead. However, a belief in prayers for the dead logically implies some sort of belief in an intermediate state independent of heaven or hell.
[265] That abuses did occur by some preachers of indulgences is no longer disputed. See, Pope Paul VI's, *Indulgentiarum Doctrina*, Apostolic

Constitution: Revision of Sacred Indulgences (Jan. 1, 1967), Chs. 4, 8, vatican.va/content/paul-vi/en/apost_constitutions/documents/hf_p-vi_apc_01011967_indulgentiarum-doctrina.html.
Because abuses did occur, even though the Church did not endorse them, it bears some responsibility for them.

[266] The attribution to St. Augustine was made a Catholic priest and one-time university professor during a lecture on Church history. I have been unable to validate its source. Regardless of its authenticity, it strikes me as profoundly true.

[267] John Paul II, *Incarnationis Mysterium,* Bull of Indiction of the Great Jubilee of the Year 2000, Nov. 29, 1998.

Pope Benedict XVI, *Urbis Et Orbis,* Apostolic Penitentiary: Decree, During the Year of Faith, special acts of penance will be rewarded with the gift of Sacred Indulgences, Sep 14, 2012, vatican.va/roman_curia/tribunals/apost_penit/documents/rc_trib_appen_doc_20120914_annus-fidei_en.html.

Pope Francis, *Decree for Plenary Indulgence on the Occasion of the Second World Day of Grandparents and the Elderly,* Mar 30, 2022, press.vatican.va/content/salastampa/en/bollettino/pubblico/2022/05/30/220530c.html.

[268] Rahner, *Theological Investigations: Man in the Church*, 194-195.

[269] *CCC,* 1471.

[270] Philosophical and theological conundrums associated with plenary indulgences are discussed in the last section of this chapter.

[271] For only God can judge the sincerity of heart in penitents seeking indulgences for themselves or for the deceased. See Pope Paul VI, *Indulgentiarum Doctrina*, Chs. 4, 11: "For indulgences cannot be acquired without a sincere conversion of mentality ('metanoia') and unity with God, to which the performance of the prescribed works is added."

[272] The Catholic Church, *Manual of Indulgences: Norms and Grants,* trans. from 4th ed, (1999) *Enchiridion Indulgentiarum* (Washington D.C., USCCB, 2006), N7.

[273] The Church asserts that the pope's power comes directly from Christ to Peter (the first pope). In Matthew 16:18-19, Jesus calls out Peter's unique and authoritative role as a leader among the apostles, making him the first pope. The Church claims her authority to forgive sins is based on the power given by Christ to his apostles after his resurrection in John 20:21b-23. The Church teaches that the Apostles passed this gift down to the priests through the Sacrament of Holy Orders and is the source of forgiveness granted by God through the Sacrament of Reconciliation. The priest acts in the person of Christ.

[274] Paul VI, *Indulgentiarum Doctrina*, Chs. 4, 7.
[275] Rahner, *Theological Investigations: Man in the Church*, 188, footnote 5.
[276] Paul VI, *Indulgentiarum Doctrina*, Norms, 13.
[277] For example, in the early Church, public penance for grave (mortal) sins could take ten years to complete before the penitent would be allowed back in full communion with his worship community. The community might assume part of the penance if the penitent had died before completing his penance.
[278] Catherine O'Connell-Cahill, "What is the Communion of Saints?" *U.S. Catholic*, Vol. 79, No. 12 (2014): 46.
[279] *CCC*, 1475.
[280] Paul VI, *Indulgentiarum Doctrina*, Chs. 2, 5.
[281] John Paul II, *General Audience*, Sep. 29, 1999, vatican.va/content/john-paul-ii/en/audiences/1999/documents/hf_jp-ii_aud_29091999.html.
[282] Jugie, S.J., *The Truth about Purgatory*, 18.
[283] Rahner, *Theological Investigations: Man in the Church*, 198.
[284] Neil Judisch, "Indulgent Love," *Purgatory: Philosophical Dimensions*, Kindle (Cham, Switzerland: Palgrave Macmillan, 2017), 98.
[285] *CCC*, 1472. A quick inventory of websites produces conflicting statements. Some sites assert that plenary indulges only reduce the time in purgatory because the temporal punishment of sins is wiped out, while other sites claim immediate purification occurs and the soul immediately is in heaven.
[286] Since indulgences do not forgive the guilt of sin before God, the Protestant position assumes that guilt of sin has already been forgiven by asking for God's forgiveness prior to death or *sola fides* must be assumed to effect forgiveness automatically.
[287] In 2009, the *New York Times* ran an article stating that the fact that "many Catholics under 50 have never sought one [an indulgence] and never heard of indulgences except in high school European history, simply makes their reintroduction more urgent among church leaders bent on restoring fading traditions of penance in what they see as a self-satisfied world." In Chapter 10, we look at the history of indulgences and their importance in "igniting" the Protestant Reformation and in the wholesale rejection of purgatory of many Christians to this day. Source: Paul Vitello, "For Catholics, a Door to Absolution Is Reopened," *New York Times*, Feb 9, 2009, nytimes.com/2009/02/10/nyregion/10indulgence.html.
[288] *Manual of Indulgences: Norms and Grants*, N1.
[289] When a priest grants an Apostolic Blessing (Pardon) to a person on their deathbed, as discussed in Chapter 11, he is granting an indulgence

authorized by papal authority.

[290] The Catholic Church, *Manual of Indulgences: Norms and Grants*, trans from 4th ed, (1999) *Enchiridion Indulgentiarum* (Washington D.C., USCCB, 2006).

[291] Mark Brumley, "Why the Reformation Was Necessary—But Protestantism Was Not," (San Diego: Catholic Answers, 2017), catholic.com/magazine/print-edition/why-the-reformation-was-necessary-but-protestantism-was-not.

Chapter 9

[292] Paul VI, *Indulgentiarum Doctrina*, 8.

[293] Marcel Metzger, trans. Madeleine Beaumont, *History of the Liturgy: The Major Stages*, Kindle (Collegeville, MI: The Liturgical Press, 1997), Ch.. 3, subsection "The Reconciliation of Penitents."

[294] St. Cyprian, trans. Maurice Bevenot, S.J., *The Lapsed: The Unity of the Catholic Church*, No. 25 in the *Ancient Christian Writers: The Works of the Fathers in Translation* (Westminster, MA: The Newman Press, 1957), 15.

[295] St. Cyprian, *The Lapsed*, 27.

[296] St. Cyprian, *The Lapsed*, 42.

[297] Jesson, "Paradise Regained," 4.

[298] St. Cyprian, *The Lapsed*, 42.

[299] Fr. Enrico dal Covolo, SDB., "The Historical Origin of Indulgences," Vatican, May 19, 1999, Sec. 1. Introduction. Originally published in *L'Osservatore Roman*, 9-10, catholicculture.org/culture/library/view.cfm?recnum=1054.

[300] My terminology "proto-indulgence" is used to distinguish between the indulgences granted prior to the Council of Clermont (1095) and those afterward.

[301] Paul Chevedden, "Canon 2 of the Council of Clermont (1095) and the Crusade Indulgence," *Annuarium Historiae Conciliorum*. 37(2) (2005), 258, researchgate.net/publication/304783738.

[302] Will Durant, *The Age of Faith* (New York: Simon and Schuster, 1950), 588.

[303] Will Durant, *The Age of Faith*, 588.

[304] Pope Leo IV's quote is cited by Chevedden, "Canon 2 of the Council of Clermont (1095) and the Crusade Indulgence. 259. See footnote 18 for the original Latin and Chevedden's primary source.

[305] Pope John VIII's letter is cited by Chevedden, "Canon 2 of the Council of Clermont (1095) and the Crusade Indulgence," 260-261. See footnote 20 for the original Latin and Chevedden's primary source.

[306] The excerpt of Pope Alexander II's address is cited by Chevedden,

"Canon 2 of the Council of Clermont (1095) and the Crusade Indulgence," 279. See footnote 56 for the original Latin and Chevedden's primary source.

[307] Cited by Chevedden, "Canon 2 of the Council of Clermont (1095) and the Goal of the Eastern Crusade," 58. See footnote 1 for the original Latin and Chevedden's primary source.

[308] This is the thesis of Paul Chevedden article, "Canon 2 of the Council of Clermont (1095), and the Goal of the Eastern Crusade."

[309] Robert W. Shaffern, "The Pardoner's Promises: Preaching and Policing Indulgences in the Fourteenth-Century English Church." *The Historian*, Vol. 68, No. 1, (Spring 2006): 50.

[310] Gregory X and Council Fathers, "Second Council of Lyons–1274," *Papal Encyclicals Online*, Constitution 1, para. 3, papalencyclicals.net/councils/ecum14.htm.

[311] Canonical penance is that penance prescribed by the confessor during the Sacrament of Reconciliation (Confession).

[312] Le Goff, *The Birth of Purgatory*, 254.

[313] Aquinas, *Summa Theologica*, 6471 (Sup III q 25 a2, *sed contra*).

[314] Rahner, *Theological Investigations: Man in the Church*, 183.

[315] Clement VI, From the Bull of Jubilee, "*Unigenitus Dei Filius*," Jan. 25, 1343. Source is Denzinger, *The Sources of Catholic Dogma*, 550-552.

[316] Shaffern, "The Pardoner's Promises: Preaching and Policing Indulgences in the Fourteenth-Century English Church," 49.

[317] Clement VI, From the letter *Super quibusdam* to the Consolator, the Catholicon of the Armenians, Sept. 20, 1351. Source: Denzinger, *The Sources of Catholic Dogma*, 570k.

[318] Summarization of William H. Kent, "Indulgences," *The Catholic Encyclopedia: An International Work Of Reference On The Constitution Doctrines Discipline And History Of The Catholic Church Vol. VII*, ed. Charles G. Herbermann, et. al. (New York: Robert Appleton Company, 1910), 787(col. 1).

[319] William H. Kent, "Indulgences," 787 (col. 2). For a detailed history of abuses, see pp. 786-788.

[320] Fr. Enrico dal Covolo, S.D.B., "The Historical Origin of Indulgences," *Trinity Publications - Catholic Culture*, Sec. 6, catholicculture.org/culture/library/view.cfm?recnum=1054.

[321] Kevin Di Camillo, "How Bad Were 'the Bad Popes?'" *National Catholic Register*, Nov. 26, 2019, ncregister.com/blog/how-bad-were-the-bad-popes.

[322] Boniface VIII, from the Bull "*Unam Sanctam*," Nov. 18, 1302. Source: Denzinger, *The Sources of Catholic Dogma*, 467.

[323] Sixtus IV, from the Bull in favor of the Church of St. Peter of Xancto, Aug. 3, 1476, Source: Denzinger, *The Sources of Catholic Dogma*, 723a.
[324] Rev. John Trigillo, Jr., PhD, ThD, and Rev Kenneth Brighenti, PhD, *Catholicism for Dummies* (Hoboken, NJ: John Wiley & Sons, 2011), 376.
[325] Leo X, In his Bull *"Cum postquan1"* to the Legate Cajetan de Vio, Nov. 9, 1518. Source: Denzinger, *The Sources of Catholic Dogma*, 740a.
[326] Shaffern, "The Pardoner's Promises: Preaching and Policing Indulgences in the Fourteenth-Century English Church," 50.
[327] Innocent III and Council Fathers, Canon 62 of *Cum ex eo*: "Medieval Sourcebook: Twelfth Ecumenical Council: Lateran IV 1215," *Internet History Sourcebooks Project, Fordham University*, Canon 62, sourcebooks.fordham.edu/basis/lateran4.asp.
[328] Shaffern, "The Pardoner's Promises: Preaching and Policing Indulgences in the Fourteenth-Century English Church," 57-58.
[329] During the Middle Ages, some men became priests due to a) lack of inheritance (which went to the first-born son) or b) dislike of military service (or knighthood) rather than a true vocation to the priesthood. Some canons of the Lateran Council (1215) paint a rather bleak picture of the quality and spirituality of the priests during the Middle Ages. Issues such as incompetence, lack of chastity, passing of clerical offices to illegitimate sons, drunkenness, and general lack of virtue are mentioned. For examples, see Canons 14-17, 27, 31. Source: *Internet History Sourcebooks Project, Fordham University*, sourcebooks.fordham.edu/basis/lateran4.asp.
[330] See Chapter IX, of the Twenty-first Session of the council of Trent (Jul. 16, 1562), ewtn.com/catholicism/library/twentyfirst-session-of-the-council-of-trent-1488.
[331] William H. Kent, "Indulgences," 787 (col. 2).
[332] For more information, see H.J. Schroeder, O.P., "The Church and the Abuse of Indulgences in the Middle Ages" in *American Catholic Quarterly Review*, XLVI (1921), 177-205. Pages 197-203 detail the pressure some unscrupulous bishops exerted on the priests and laity.
[333] Paul VI, *Indulgentiarum Doctrina*, 8. Internal quotes contain an extract from the Council of Trent (Denzinger, 1835).
[334] Martin Luther's *Ninety-Five Theses* (1517) contain 15 grievances mentioning purgatory and 35 listing abuses of indulgences.
[335] Phillip Goyret, "Luther's 95 Theses: A Catholic Approach," Služba Božja (Divine Service), 2018, 58/2, 210-224.
[336] Martin Luther, "Luther's 95 Thesis - 1517," *Internet Archive*, 26, archive.org/details/95ThesesMartinLuther.
[337] Faith alone, Scripture alone, Christ alone, Grace alone, respectively.
[338] Martin Luther, "The Smalcald Articles - 1537," *Gutenberg Project*, Second

Part, Article II, gutenberg.org/files/273/273-h/273-h.htm.
[339] Lutheran-Catholic Dialogue, "Hope of Eternal Life," 2010, 181.
[340] Lutheran-Catholic Dialogue, "Hope of Eternal Life," 2010, 191, which I have summarized.
[341] John Calvin, trans. by Henry Beveridge, *Institutes of the Christian Religion*, Chapter 5, Article 6, 562.
[342] Calvin, *Institutes of the Christian Religion*, 559.
[343] Pius IV and the Council Fathers, "Twenty-Fifth Session of the Council of Trent," Dec. 4, 1563, Chapter XXI, ewtn.com/catholicism/library/twentyfifth-session-of-the-council-of-trent-1492.
[344] However, Luther ended this section on "Prayer for the Dead" with this sentence: "For vigils and requiem masses and yearly celebrations of requiems are useless, and are merely the devil's annual fair." See wolfmueller.co/the-third-part-of-martin-luthers-great-confession-concerning-christs-supper-1528/.
[345] William Holden Harrington and John Wesley, *Wesley in Company with High Churchmen* (London: J. Hodges, 1872), 84-87.
[346] Lewis, *Letters to Malcolm*, 107.
[347] Benedict XVI, *Spe Salvi*, 48.

Chapter 10

[348] Jugie, *The Truth about Purgatory*, 133.
[349] Walls, *Purgatory: The Logic of Total Transformation*, 90-91.
[350] Judisch, "Sanctification, Satisfaction, and the Purpose of Purgatory," 167-185.
[351] Masters of Zwder van Culemborg, Souls in Purgatory (column miniature), *Missal of Eberhard von Greiffenklau* (c. 1425-1450), (W. 174, folio 168v, Sec. Votive Masses), The Walters Art Museum, Baltimore, MD. CC0 1.0 Universal (CC0 1.0), Public Domain. See manuscript at manuscripts.thewalters.org/viewer.php?id=W.174#page/342/mode/2up.
[352] Credit goes to Rev. Matthew O'Leary, PhD, who was able to decipher the Latin words in this image. He wrote that the closest translations now used liturgically are "Have mercy on me, God, in accord with your merciful love" or "Have mercy on me, O God, according to thy steadfast love." (cf. Psalm 51.1) My Latin to English translation is via Google Translate.
[353] Jennifer Healy, "Souls in Purgatory, Missal of Eberhard von Greiffenklau (c. 1425–1450)." *Catholic Education Resource Center*, 2019. Originally published in *Magnificat* (Nov. 2019), catholiceducation.org/en/culture/art/souls-in-purgatory-missal-of-

eberhard-von-greiffenklau-c-1425-1450.html.
[354] J.P. Arendzen, DD, *Purgatory and Heaven* (Rockford, IL: TAN Books and Publishers, 1960), 27.
[355] Margaret Crable, "Why Dante and his 'Divine Comedy' remain relevant 700 years after his death," *University of Southern California Dornslif*, Sep. 13, 2021, dornsife.usc.edu/news/stories/dante-devine-comedy-still-relevant/(sic).
[356] Alfonso de Salvio, "Heterodoxy in Dante's Purgatory." *PMLA* 38, no. 1 (1923), 71 and 74.
[357] Le Goff, *The Birth of Purgatory*, 334.
[358] Phillip A. Wicksteed, *Dante and Aquinas* (New York: E. P. Dutton & Co., 1913), 232-233.
[359] This opinion is expressed by most Protestant philosophers, who are open to purgatory as a place of sanctification but take great pains to emphasize that their purgatory is not the Catholic purgatory which includes temporal punishment for sins. Quoted phrases from Jerry Walls, *Purgatory: The Logic of Total Transformation*, 90-91.
[360] M. F. Egan, S. J., "The Two Theories of Purgatory," *Irish Theological Quarterly*, 17 (1922), 24.
[361] Egan, "The Two Theories of Purgatory," 28.
[362] I am not a good example of this statement. Nevertheless, Schouppe's *Purgatory: Explained by the Lives and Legends of the Saints* is one of the first books that I purchased and read when I began my research on purgatory.
[363] Schouppe, *Purgatory: Explained by the Lives and Legends of the Saints*, 163.
[364] Schouppe, *Purgatory: Explained by the Lives and Legends of the Saints*, xxxv.
[365] Schouppe, *Purgatory: Explained by the Lives and Legends of the Saints*, xxxvi.
[366] Gerard J. M. Van Den Aardweg, *Hungry Souls: Supernatural Visits, Messages and Warnings from Purgatory* (Charlotte, NC: TAN Books, 2012), 45-47.
[367] Saint Gertrude the Great, *The Life and Revelations of Saint Gertrude* (New York: Catholic Publication Society, 1870). Many examples are found in Sec. V, including those on pages 522, 525-526, 532.
[368] Catherine of Genoa, trans. Serge Hughes, et al., *Catherine of Genoa: Purgation and Purgatory, The Spiritual Dialogue (Classics of Western Spirituality)* (Mahwah, NJ: Paulist Press, 1979), 1-2.
[369] Catherine of Genoa, *Catherine of Genoa: Purgation and Purgatory*, 64-65.
[370] St. Catherine of Genoa, *Fire of Love: Understanding Purgatory* (Manchester, NH: Sophia Institute Press, 1996), 63.
[371] Saint Teresa of Avila, trans. Kieran Kavanaugh OCD, Otilio Rodríguez, *The Autobiography of St. Teresa of Avila* (New York: Book-of-the-Month Club (One Spirit), 1995). Examples may be found on pages 142,

178, 179, 268, 302, 313, 340, 341, 342, and 344.
[372] Saint Teresa of Avila, *The Autobiography of St. Teresa of Avila*, 313.
[373] Casimir Krzyzanowski, MIC, *The Illustrated Story of Saint Stanislaus Papczynski* (Stockbridge, MA Marian Press: 2016), 81.
[374] "The Marians' Founder, Stanislaus Papczyński, is Canonized," *Marian Fathers of the Immaculate Conception of the BVM*, Jun. 6, 2016, thedivinemercy.org/articles/marians-founder-stanislaus-papczynski-canonized.
[375] Bernard Ruffin, *Padre Pio, the True Story* (Huntington, IN: Our Sunday Visitor, 1982), 135-136.
[376] Saint Maria Faustina Kowalska, *Divine Mercy in My Soul*, Kindle (Stockbridge, MA: Marian Press, 2014), 58.
[377] Kowalska, *Divine Mercy in My Soul*, 58.
[378] Kowalska, *Divine Mercy in My Soul*, 20.
[379] Anther resource for more information on the Divine Mercy Chaplet and St. Faustina is Meggie K. Daly, *For the Sake of His Sorrowful Passion: Praying the Divine Mercy Chaplet with Scripture and Art* (USA: Misericordia Publishing, 2020).
[380] Kowalska, *Divine Mercy in My Soul*, 1226.
[381] Kowalska, *Divine Mercy in My Soul*, 1227.
[382] See *CCC*, 67.
[383] Arendzen, *Purgatory and Heaven*, 30.

Chapter 11

[384] Hans Urs von Balthazar, *Who is a Christian?* (Westminster, Md: Newman Press, 1967), 78.
[385] My restatement of article 45 in Pope Benedict XVI's *Spe Salvi*.
[386] Benedict XVI, *Spe Salvi*, 46.
[387] Jugie, *The Truth about Purgatory*, 132-133.
[388] Jugie, *The Truth about Purgatory*, 141-169.
[389] Viaticum is the name given to that last reception of the Eucharist as the dying pass from this life *en route* to the Father and united with the Son. For more information, see *CCC*, 1524-1525.
[390] *CCC*, 1521-1523.
[391] See the *Manual of Indulgences: Norms and Grants*, Grants 12 §§1-4, (pp. 54-55). "If a priest is unavailable, Holy Mother Church benevolently grants to the Christian faithful, who are duly disposed, a plenary indulgence to be acquired at the point of death, provided they have been in the habit of reciting some prayers during their lifetime; in such a case, the Church supplies for the three conditions ordinarily required for a

plenary indulgence" (12 §§2).
[392] The conundrum of plenary indulgences was touched upon in Chapter 8 in the section entitled "Further Reflections and Open Questions." *CCC* 1472 states that purification frees one of the temporal punishment due to sin and that this purification must take place either in this life or in purgatory. For me, a plenary indulgence is a mysterious fusion of divine mercy and justice. I have to side with St. Augustine, St. Anselm of Canterbury, and St. Bernard of Clairvaux—all of whom had some rendition of "*I believe that I may understand.*"
[393] Susan Tassone, *Prayers, Promises, and Devotions for the Holy Souls in Purgatory* (Huntington, IN: Our Sunday Visitor, 2012), 186.
[394] Jugie, *The Truth about Purgatory*, 179-206.
[395] Rev. Johann Roten, SM, "Our Lady of Mount Carmel Brown Scapular," *All About Mary*, University of Dayton, udayton.edu/imri/mary/o/our-lady-of-mount-carmel-scapular.php.
[396] Schouppe, *Purgatory: Explained by the Lives and Legends of the Saints*, 366-367.
[397] For more information on Sabbatine privilege, see "Sabbatine Privilege," *New Advent Encyclopedia*, newadvent.org/cathen/13289b.htm.
[398] Congregation for Divine Worship and the Discipline of the Sacraments, *Directory on Popular Piety and the Liturgy. Principles and Guidelines.* (Vatican, Dec. 2001), 205, vatican.va/roman_curia/congregations/ccdds/documents/rc_con_ccdds_doc_20020513_vers-direttorio_en.html.
[399] Suggested resources to dig a bit deeper into Marian Consecration: *Total Consecration to Jesus through Mary* by St. Louis de Montfort; *33 Days to Morning Glory* by Michael E. Gaitley, MIC; and for Pope St. John Paul II, see Leo Cardinal Scheffczyk, "The Systematic Aspect of Marian Consecration in Life and Teaching of John Paul II," *All About Mary*, University of Dayton, udayton.edu/imri/mary/p/pope-john-paul-ii-and-consecration-to-mary.php.
[400] Jugie, *The Truth about Purgatory*, 191.
[401] Conrad De Meester, OCD, *The Power of Confidence*, 2nd Edition (Staten Island, NY: Alba House, 1995), 361-365.
[402] Saint Thérèse de Lisieux, translated by Thomas N. Taylor, *The Story of a Soul (L'Histoire d'une Âme): The Autobiography of St. Thérèse of Lisieux With additional Writings and Sayings of St. Thérèse.* (Hamburg: Tredition, 2005), 44.
[403] Saint Thérèse, *The Story of a Soul*, 111.
[404] Fr. Michael E. Gaitley, MIC, *33 Days to Merciful Love: A Do-It-Yourself Retreat in Preparation for Consecration to Divine Mercy* (Stockbridge, MA: Marian Press, 2016), 80.

[405] Quoted by De Meester, *The Power of Confidence*, 348. His original reference is St. Thérèse of Lisieux, trans, John Clarke OCD, *Her Last Conversations*, (Washington, D.C., ICS, 1977).
[406] Saint Thérèse, *The Story of a Soul*, 267-269.
[407] Gaitley, *33 Days to Merciful Love*, 81.
[408] Saint Thérèse, *The Story of a Soul*, 267-269.
[409] Saint Thérèse, *The Story of a Soul*, 269.
[410] Saint Thérèse, *The Story of a Soul*, 113.
[411] Purification by purgatorial fires was often used literally or figuratively for centuries by religious people, even though "fire" is not included in the dogmatic statements of the Church. Fire was often alluded to based on 1 Corinthians 3:11-15 as we saw in Chapter 7.
[412] St. John of the Cross, trans. David Lewis, *The Dark Night of the Soul* (London: Thomas Baker, 1908), 18, 88, 110.
[413] Saint Thérèse, *The Story of a Soul*, 274.
[414] Saint Thérèse, *The Story of a Soul*, 163.
[415] Saint Thérèse, *The Story of a Soul*, 184-185. These pages include the testimony of those who were with her when she died.

Chapter 12

[416] Lane, *Keeping Hope Alive*, 146.
[417] Stump, "Atonement and Justification," 191-195. Quoted text from the bottom of page 194.
[418] Lane, *Keeping Hope Alive*, 146.
[419] Hendzel, "An Exploration of the Roman Catholic Doctrine of Purgatory in Light of Current Issues in Theodicy," 9.
[420] Hendzel, "An Exploration of the Roman Catholic Doctrine of Purgatory in Light of Current Issues in Theodicy," 14.
[421] John Paul II, *Evangelium Vitae*, Encyclical: Value and Inviolability of Human Life (Gospel of Life), Mar 25, 1995, 67, vatican.va/content/john-paul-ii/en/encyclicals/documents/hf_jp-ii_enc_25031995_evangelium-vitae.html.
[422] Kowalska, *Divine Mercy in My Soul*, 57.
[423] Saint Thérèse, *The Story of a Soul*, 183.
[424] De Meester, *The Power of Confidence*, 286-287
[425] Saint Thérèse, *The Story of a Soul*, 51.
[426] Saint Thérèse, *The Story of a Soul*, 203.
[427] Saint Thérèse, *The Story of a Soul*, 203.
[428] Balthazar, *Dare We Hope "That All Men Be Saved?"* 123.
[429] John Paul II, General Audience, August 4, 1999, vatican.va/content/john-paul-ii/en/audiences/1999/documents/hf_jp-

ii_aud_04081999.html.
[430] CCC, 2094.
[431] Novello, "Eschatology since Vatican II: Saved in hope," 423.
[432] Novello, "Eschatology since Vatican II: Saved in hope," 423.
[433] Saint Augustine, trans. Maria Boulding, OSB, ed John Rotelle, OSA, *The Confessions* (Hyde Park, NY: New City Press, 1997), 137 (Book VIII, first two sentences).

www.ingramcontent.com/pod-product-compliance
Lightning Source LLC
Chambersburg PA
CBHW061737070526
44585CB00024B/2703